THE RAFT FISHERMEN

INDIANA UNIVERSITY LATIN AMERICAN SERIES

by *Shepard Forman*

THE RAFT FISHERMEN

*Tradition & Change in the Brazilian
Peasant Economy*

Indiana University Press / *Bloomington & London*
for International Affairs Center

HN
283.5
F6

The section entitled "Cognition and the Catch" in Chapter V is based on Professor Forman's article in *Ethnology* VI(4):417–26, and is printed here with the permission of its publisher.

TO MY PARENTS
SIMON AND ANN FORMAN

Contents

PREFACE   xi

I. INTRODUCTION   3
The Geography of Raft Fishing   6
The History of Raft Fishing   10

II. THE COMMUNITY: COQUEIRAL   17
The Setting   17
History   17
Topography and Land Use   21
Economic Organization in the County   26
Migration   28
Communication   31

III. SOCIAL STRUCTURE AND THE
PEASANT ECONOMY   34

IV. STRATIFICATION AND
PRODUCTIVE TECHNOLOGY   46
Beach Seine   47
Lambuda   52
Caceia   53
Other Fishing Techniques   55
Subsistence Fishing   57
Subsistence and Entrepreneurship   57

V. THE NATURE OF RAFT FISHING   61
Cognition and the Catch   65
Production   74

VI. DISTRIBUTION AND REDISTRIBUTION 81

VII. PATTERNS OF OWNERSHIP 93

VIII. CREDIT, CAPITAL, AND SAVINGS 105

IX. INNOVATION AND CHANGE 118

X. CONCLUSION 131

BIBLIOGRAPHY 139

NOTES 145

INDEX 153

Illustrations

PHOTOGRAPHS

Raft fishing on the high seas   i
Coconut harvester at work in Coqueiral   25
A street in the village   35
Shore crew hauling in a pocket seine   49
Baiting for shrimp with a dip net   59
Complete tool kit for jangada construction   95
Carpenter joining the logs of a new jangada   95
Woman weaving a straw basket. Her wares are
    displayed in the window.   113

FIGURES

1. A Typical Jangada   2
2. Seasonal Fishing Patterns   63
3. Sample Extended-Family Network   107

MAPS

I. County of Guaiamu   18
II. Local Land Use and Topography   20
III. Fishing Grounds (vicinity of Coqueiral)   69
IV. Northeast Fishing Zone   120–121

Tables

1. Occupational Distribution of Males and Females in Coqueiral 27
2. Occupational Distribution of Heads of Households in Coqueiral 28
3. Emigration from Coqueiral of Males and Females with Relatives Remaining in the Village 29
4. Emigration from Coqueiral of Males with Relatives Remaining in the Village 30
5. Income and Expenditures of the Côlonia de Pescadores Antônio Barnabé 42
6. Income and Fringe Benefits of the Côlonia de Pescadores Antônio Barnabé 43
7. Sample Distribution of Beach Seine Catch 51
8. Production Statistics for Raft Fishing with Two Gill Nets 54
9. Production Statistics for Sample One-Month Periods of Four Rafts in Coqueiral 76
10. Wholesale and Retail Prices of Fish [in Coqueiral and Guaiamu] 88
11. Wholesale and Retail Prices of Fish Sold at Usina Boa Fé and Palmeira 89
12. Number of Rafts According to Fishing Season 94
13. Prices of Jangada Parts and Accoutrements in Coqueiral 96
14. Prices of Hooks and Line in Coqueiral 98
15. Expenditures for Food and Fuel 98
16. Fish Taken for Home Consumption 99
17. Differential Earnings of Owners and Crew for Sample One-Month Period 100
18. Earnings and Debts of Pensioner's Family 109

Preface

MY INTEREST in Brazilian fishing villages began in the year 1961-62, when I first went to Brazil as a Fulbright grantee. Although I travelled extensively throughout the country, I continually found myself drawn back to the coast. There was, obviously, the natural attraction of Brazil's beautiful tropical beaches. There was also the fact that fishermen are willing informants. They are always available for conversation on the beach, and they like nothing better than to have an anthropologist as an apprentice fisherman.

I returned to Brazil in 1963 as Graduate Assistant to the Columbia-Cornell-Harvard-Illinois Summer Field Studies Program, which offers training in ethnographic research to undergraduates in the participating universities. A number of coastal communities in the state of Bahia were used as field stations. I was located in a village that specializes in hook-and-line fishing from hull sailboats (Kottak 1966). However, I was aware from my previous experience that other types of fishing craft, particularly log rafts, predominated in similar areas of the northeast coast, a region which could be defined by its distinct physiography.

In December, 1964, I again returned to Brazil in order to study the fishing economy in the northeastern part of the country. I was particularly interested in mapping the spread and distribution of predominant fishing techniques before starting on a comparative study of ecological variation and social organization in three communities specializing in log rafts, canoes, or hull sailboats. A firsthand examination of conditions along the coast south of Salvador in the states of Bahia and Espirito Santo had convinced me that the geographic limits of log-raft fishing coincided with the Northeast as a single physiographic region—the Northeast Fishing Zone. While extremely difficult travel conditions and limitations of time and money precluded a personal visit to the area north of Fortaleza, discussion with members of the Fisheries Development Organization (Grupo de Desenvolvimento de Pesca) in Ceará and with the Director of the Institute of Marine Biology of the Universidade de Ceará satisfied me as to the northern limits of the area in question. In addition, published reports of conditions in northern Ceará and in the states of Piauí and Maranhão confirmed my impression that the type of fishing done in this region best fitted an Amazonian classification in which canoe fishing with nets on rivers and estuaries predominated (Coelho 1963, Albuquerque 1961). Accordingly, from February to April, 1965, I visited fishing villages along the Brazilian coast from Salvador, in the state of Bahia, north to Fortaleza, in Ceará. This coastal survey took into account the location, size, harbor conditions, economic resources, productive technology, and market network of a variety of communities in Northeast Brazil.

What emerged finally from the coastal survey was a new hypothesis concerning technological change, which then became the basis for my study. As I viewed the map on which the data from my survey had been recorded (see Map IV), a certain pattern of technological change became evident. It appeared that a switch from the use of log rafts to hull sailboats in coastal fishing was associated with three rather specific variables. First, the change was instigated by particular marketable species of fish which could be exploited for a consumer market. Second, the fishing ports in which such change took place were located near and in communication with large urban markets. Third, their great distance from the source of logs used in the manufacture of rafts raised the cost of rafts beyond the peasants' means to purchase them.

In order to examine these contentions, a study of the fishing economy and its organization on the community level was essential, since it was there that the multiple elements involved in the maintenance of a traditional economy could be carefully scrutinized. For this purpose I selected a coastal fishing village that appeared to represent the most traditional aspects of the fishing economy in Northeast Brazil, and I devoted seven months, from April to November, 1965, to ethnographic research there. In the summer of 1967, I again returned to the same area to undertake a study of peasant marketing systems

(Forman and Riegelhaupt 1970). For all apparent purposes, the village in 1967 was exactly as I had left it in 1965; and unless otherwise noted, all tables in this book contain data collected during the 1965 field trip.

Although the present study relies primarily on the data gathered in this one community, it does not pretend in any way to be a "community study" that focuses primary attention on the understanding of the community itself as a whole. Rather, it is an attempt to approach the specific socioeconomic problem of technological innovation and change on an empirical basis, utilizing the methods of anthropology to discover and understand the processes of change within the traditional economic system. Surely, it is only with a clear conception of the cultural content of a peasant economy in its historical dimensions that conclusions can be drawn as to the *when* and *how* of technological innovation and change. While such a "life history" approach to an economic activity can best be carried out on the local level, mere study *in loco* does not provide the essential framework for an understanding of tradition and change.

Economic activities in contemporary peasant societies are not so self-contained that they can be studied in their entireties by a single anthropologist in the local community. Only by looking beyond the little community is the anthropologist likely to see the hierarchy of relationships which often determine the very nature of the local economy (Wagley and Harris 1955:433). The treatment of the village as an isolated phenomenon would surely obscure the effects of the larger, highly differentiated socio-economic system to which it is tied. Yet an analysis of organization on the village level is required to demonstrate the processes that maintain in the little community an apparently static set of dependent, reduplicative family units which operate somewhere between the traditional and modern worlds.

To this end the author has been aided by a number of institutions and individuals. Research in the field was supported by a National-Defense-Education-Act–related Fulbright-Hays award. For the coastal survey, Columbia University supplied me with a jeep and funds for its maintenance. The Penesa Company of Recife, Pernambuco, Brazil, furnished me with a driver-guide. The Brazilian Public Health Service (Serviço Especial de Saude Pública) provided me with routes of access to innumerable villages, thus adding considerable depth to the survey. SESP'S "foot soldiers" in the campaign against malaria gave me maps and census data that proved invaluable. I must also acknowledge my debt to Dr. Rene Bertholet of the Pindorama agricultural colony in the state of Alagoas and to Joop Liethoff of the Dutch Overseas Volunteers for making available the facilities of the colony for printing all the questionnaires and data sheets. Funds for the analysis of the data and support during the writing of this book were provided by a National Institutes of Mental Health Predoctoral Research Fellowship.

It is not easy to express my gratitude to Professor Charles Wagley, who supervised the research and writing of the dissertation on which this monograph is based. I am particularly indebted to Professor Marvin Harris for his careful reading of the manuscript and for his invaluable assistance. Professor Harris visited me in the village and contributed innumerable insights to both the field situation and the research in general. Dr. Joyce F. Riegelhaupt read the original draft of the manuscript and offered many helpful suggestions. I am also indebted to Mrs. Helen Schroeder for the original maps and figures in this study, which she painstakingly rendered from aerial photographs, political and topographic maps, and oceanographic charts.

I am grateful to all of my Columbia colleagues in Brazil for our exchange of ideas during three seminars in the field and for their general encouragement. Christopher Tavener joined me for nearly three months, during which time he was a welcome companion. He assisted me in the difficult task of completing a village household survey and census and in making a map of the village.

The Brazilians who helped me in my research are so numerous that I can mention only a few. Sr. Hans Greve of Salvador, Bahia, taught me much of what I know of fishing. Dr. Soloncy José Cerdeiro de Moura, of SUDENE (Agency for the Development of the Northeast), and his predecessor, Commander Thales Freire, offered me invaluable assistance. Their support of my work and their interest in the welfare of Brazilian fishermen was a constant source of encouragement. I am also grateful to Dr. Tulio Marroquim, Director of SUDEPE (Agency for the Development of Fishing) in the state of Alagoas, for his help on many occasions. Moacir Medeiros de Santana, Director of the Public

Archive in Alagoas, and Tarcisio Régo Quirino of the Brazilian Institute of Educational Research in Recife led me to the available historical resources. Sr. Tércio Wanderley and Dr. Vitor Wanderley
made it possible for me to stay in Coqueiral. Without their cooperation the study of this particular community would have been impossible. I shall never forget Dr. Theo Brandão for the help, encouragement, and friendship that he bestowed upon a lonely field worker.

Finally, the study could not have been made at all were it not for
the fishermen throughout Brazil and particularly in Coqueiral. I am
most especially grateful to José Bernardo de Santos, who served as my
field assistant. José Souza dos Santos aided me in the collection of data
on production. Dona Francisca dos Santos resolved all of the domestic
problems related to my field research. Genesio Batista dos Santos was
my *mestre de jangada,* my cicerone, and my friend. With my wife,
Leona, I share the extreme pleasure of having known them and lived
among them.

THE RAFT FISHERMEN

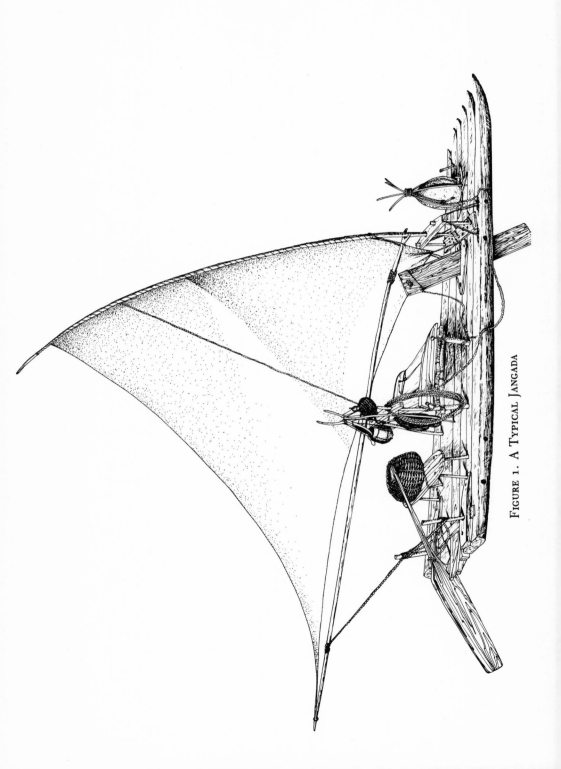

FIGURE 1. A TYPICAL JANGADA

[I]

Introduction

THE JANGADA, or log raft, is characteristic of the landscape of Northeast Brazil. Since they were first described in the accounts of the earliest travelers to the New World, these log rafts have been a source of literary curiosity. The Portuguese called them *jangadas*, adapting the name of a similar craft they had seen in their voyages to the Indies. The simple craft sailing into the wind on a tropical sea or drying on a sunny beach lined with coconut palms have made endless film footage. Raft fishermen—*jangadeiros*—have been immortalized in song and poetry. The setting for jangada fishing is truly idyllic, and the saga of the jangadeiro reads like a romantic adventure. Raft fishermen have become legendary heroes along much of the Brazilian coast, and their daring and courage are recounted across generations. The fame of some *mestre de jangada* (captain of a raft) is part of the history of every major seaport in Northeast Brazil.

Rare is the traveler to the Northeast who does not want to *passear de jangada* (go for a ride on a raft). He has heard innumerable tales about Mestre Fulano—of the huge fish he caught, of the day he capsized and righted the raft himself, and of how his raft is the very fastest on the beach. "But is it seaworthy?" the fearful tourist might ask. He will be told how much safer a jangada is than a sailboat and how Mestre Geronimo sailed his small log raft from Fortaleza to Buenos Aires. (Mestre Geronimo, the most famous of Brazilian raftsmen, was lost at sea in 1965 while fishing from his home port of Fortaleza.)

Once aboard, skimming over the surf and across the reefs onto the open sea, the tourist becomes aware of the thrill of sailing on a raft, and he quickly forgets his misgivings. He feels the coolness of the ocean as it washes over his feet and delights in the notion that he is standing in a vast expanse of sea. He is reassured by the *mestre* who

3

sits confidently on the captain's bench, steadying the oar that serves
as rudder and ably maneuvering the raft among the swells. He marvels
at the agility of the crew member who darts across the coiled anchor
rope to raise or lower the centerboard keel, to wet down the sail, or to
lift the mast against his shoulder when it is time to come about. The
passenger on the raft loses all thought of impending danger and returns to shore confident that he now understands the jangadeiro's at-
tachment to the sea and to his traditional craft. He bounds onto the
beach a happy advocate of the romantics who seek to protect the
jangada from the encroachment of modern fishing techniques.

The jangadeiros themselves know that change is inevitable, and
under some circumstances they welcome it. Hardship and danger are a
constant part of their daily fishing activities. The tourist on a *passeio*
does not spend long hours burning under the hot sun. He does not sail
into a storm, shivering in the wind and rain. His feet are not immersed
in the sea for ten or twelve hours at a time. He brings along warm clothing, which the jangadeiro usually does not have. He is probably not
aware that even in the tropics fishermen can suffer numbing pain in
their ears and hands. One fisherman insisted that he would not set sail
without a few preliminary drags on a marijuana cigarette against the
cold.

Furthermore, the recompense for fishing from a raft is very low. A
raft's total monthly catch rarely exceeds one hundred pounds of fish.
Earnings are as low as $5 a month for each member of the crew. The
reader will be struck, as I was time and again, by the small amounts of
money involved: the fishermen of Northeast Brazil deal in what we
consider to be petty sums. For the peasant producer in Brazil, however, pennies are extremely significant.[1] One penny buys a box of
matches, and ten pennies, a liter of kerosene. With fifty pennies a
family can buy a liter of beans, and $3 is a typical weekly expenditure
for food. Approximately $15 can buy a fisherman a raft and fishing
tackle.

One might well ask why they fish. What is the jangadeiro's attach-
ment to the sea and to a small log raft? Why does a man fish without
ample reward? The answer is not, as the poets would have us believe,
because the sea, wind, and salt are in his soul. He fishes simply because
there is no other opportunity open to him. Comitas (1962:18) states

that where a choice is possible, individuals prefer agriculture and wage work to fishing. Along the coast of Northeast Brazil there is very little choice, and raft fishing affords at least some steady source of protein in an otherwise scanty diet.

Then why do jangadeiros not try to improve their lot? Why do they not try to fish from more modern craft? The fishermen of the community of Coqueiral are fully aware that there are other fishing techniques and that under certain conditions these other techniques are preferable. When queried about the lack of change in their own community, however, they responded with the oft-heard comment, "*Não da aqui, não!*" (it won't work here). The reason why it won't work there is the subject of the subsequent chapters.

The bulk of fishing along the coast of Northeast Brazil is still done by hook and line from jangadas made from a light, balsa-like wood (*Apeiba tuberbou*) known as *piuba* or *pau de jangada* (jangada wood). Constructed entirely of wood and vegetable fiber and made with the simplest of tools, the jangada represents the most primitive of ocean-going craft. No metal is used because rust causes rotting. A typical jangada is made of a mere eight logs, each approximately eight meters long and one and one-half meters wide, which are held together by long wooden pegs (see Figure 1). It is propelled by a triangular sail, fastened to a simple wooden mast that is set into a step at the bow.[2] A centerboard keel descends through a keelson in the innermost logs, just in front of a simple platform, the *salgadeira*, on which fish are salted and stored. A large basket, the *samburá*, is placed under the salting platform for the storage of fresh fish, kept so by the constant flow of water over the logs. A forked staff, from which fishing line, a basket containing hooks and bait, and gourds for food and water all are suspended, is fastened between two slender uprights to the back of the salting platform. Coiled rope, leading to the rock anchor, and safety lines are attached to the uprights. A wooden bench in the stern and an oar, which serves as the rudder, are among the accoutrements of the largest rafts.

Among the many advantages of such log rafts over other craft are their easy construction, low cost, and relative stability, maneuverability, and speed. In addition, the use of prevailing offshore winds for propulsion, the ease of beaching the raft, and the facility with which the jangada passes over the low-lying reefs make it an extremely effective fishing craft for the region.

There are also disadvantages. The very properties which make jangada wood extremely buoyant also account for its being highly perishable. The wood is so light and porous that when dry it often weighs less than cork. For this reason, it quickly becomes waterlogged, and a jangada must be replaced every other year at least.

The fishermen, however, appear intent on replacing the rafts in their traditional form, not on innovation. There is, certainly, little money available for experimentation with new equipment, although mechanisms for credit and savings do exist. Still, we are not confronted with a simple case of making do with what one has, but rather with a seemingly consistent choice of the old over the new. The question to pursue is why new equipment does not supersede the old. Part of the answer lies in the fact that the entire raft is not lost at once; some accoutrements can be salvaged and used on a similar construction. Nevertheless, this does not explain why changes have been adopted in some areas along the coast but not in others. Swift (1964:155) writes:

In an industry such as fishing where the most productive forms of activity require continuous and heavy investment in nets and boats, there is scope for the man with capital to acquire control of the independent producer through capital advances, especially if the fisherman's problems are complicated by a season during which he receives very little, if any income. Control by capitalists in different degree has been the common fate of the Malay fisherman.

It has been precisely under such conditions of entrepreneurial control over independent producers that technological innovation and change has taken place in the raft-fishing industry of Northeast Brazil. In each case, a particular species of fish was being exploited for an urban consumer market, and fishermen were forced to abandon their traditional rafts because of the prohibitive prices of logs.

THE GEOGRAPHY OF RAFT FISHING

The zone fished by jangadas stretches from the southern part of the state of Bahia to the north of the city of Fortaleza, Ceará, an area which coincides with the original settlement of coastal Tupinambá Indians. Throughout the Northeast Fishing Zone, however, the traveler encounters coastal settlements which specialize in various kinds of fishing activity (see Map IV). Generally speaking, fishing in Northeast Brazil is of three different types. The first, *pesca litoranea* (onshore fishing), takes place primarily in rivers and estuaries, bays and lagoons. It is characterized by dugout or plank canoes. Cast nets, dip nets, and beach seines are utilized, as well as a number of fixed devices such as weirs, corrals, and fish-breeding tanks. The second type, *pesca costeira* (coastal fishing), takes place in the waters above the continental shelf. Coastal fishing, the primary concern of this study, is characterized by log rafts of varying sizes and by small sailboats. Handlines, dip nets, pots, and drift nets predominate in coastal fishing. Both demersal and pelagic species are caught by these methods, although the latter are far more common. The third kind of fishing, *pesca oceanica* (ocean fishing), using large vessels to capture pelagic or demersal species of fish with various trawl nets or long lines, is not very well developed in Brazil, although it dates from colonial times when whales were hunted in the area. The principal development of late comes from Japanese fishing vessels exploring the tuna banks off the coast.

While the fishing economy of Northeast Brazil is underdeveloped by any measure, certain changes have taken place. In ports closest to urban zones, many of the indigenous dugouts have been replaced by plank canoes. On other beaches, log rafts have been replaced by facsimiles made of planks and having storage facilities in the narrow hold formed in the hull. These plank rafts, called *jangadas de tabua,* follow the same principle of design and function much in the same way as the traditional log rafts.

In still other areas along the northeast coast, European fishing boats are found. Portuguese-style hull sailboats with closed decks predominate in southern Pernambuco state, in northern Alagoas, and in the northern part of the state of Rio Grande do Norte. A smaller, open-hull sailboat, also of Portuguese derivation and called a *saveiro,* is found in the area just around the city of Salvador. Undoubtedly, the difference in these two types of fishing vessels reflects certain ecological factors. The continental shelf in the area of Salvador is only about seven miles in width, as opposed to some twenty miles along the coast of the state of Pernambuco and more in the vicinity of Rio Grande do Norte. The greater traveling distance to the fishing grounds in the north requires both a larger craft, capable of sailing over greater distances and staying out for several days, and a covered deck for sleeping and the storage of fish.

Neither cultural origins nor physical conditions alone account for the spread and distribution of boat types along the coast of Northeast Brazil. In his well-known work, *Culture and Conquest: America's Spanish Heritage* (1960:100), George Foster writes that there is a screening process at work in the transfer of cultural elements from a dominant to a subordinate group and that not all of the cultural repertoire of the dominant group is automatically transferred to the recipient culture. The basis for such selectivity is found either in the stock of equipment available to the culture carrier or in the discretion exercised by the recipient peoples (*Ibid.*, 227). Those items selected earliest "crystallize" in the colonial culture, which henceforth becomes less receptive to change (*Ibid.*, 232–33). In an attempt to modify Foster's diffusionist model of culture change, Hammel and Haase (n.d.) surveyed a series of villages along the Peruvian coast. Their discussion of the persistence of indigenous types of craft makes note that these are adequate as a means of subsistence but not for commercial production. They then point out that the degree of modernity in the Peruvian fishing industry correlates closely with the degree of commercialization (*Ibid.*, 223). Had the authors stopped here, even such a simple modification in Foster's thesis would have brought us a good deal closer to an understanding of technological innovation and change. Yet, the authors proceed to correlate the degree of modernity and commercialization in the fishing industry with the area of greatest outside influence. Contact is still the essential factor in the adoption of new techniques.

Certainly the successful diffusion of fishing techniques in Brazil cannot be explained solely on the basis of culture contact. Portugal has long been advanced in the art of fishing. Portuguese fishermen form the backbone of the fishing industry in Cape Cod, Massachusetts, and fishermen from the Azores brought essentially modern fishing techniques to southern Brazil (Bernardes 1959). However, initial contact was

made with Northeast Brazil, and Portuguese influence was more inten-
sive there for the first three centuries of her colonial settlement. Selectivity in the diffusion of fishing techniques in Northeast Brazil can be
understood only by analyzing the economic and ecological pressures at
play in that region. Lagos (1961:130) notes that a large consumer
market has stimulated innovation in the fishing industry in southern
Brazil. Richardson (1962:43) explains further:

The richer [fishing] grounds are said to be in the south, in the Falkland
current which pushes north along the Patagonian shelf, with the particularly rich grounds lying at the confluence of these currents, somewhere
approximately at the latitude of the River Plate. It is in the southern
part of Brazil that finance is available for fishing and that the greatest
density of human population is found.

Generally speaking, types of fishing craft have been adopted to meet
specific ecological and economic conditions, both marine and terres-
trial. The results of my coastal survey yield three correlations with
regard to the switch from the indigenous log raft to Portuguese-style
hull sailboats in various parts of the Northeast. First, wherever such a
change has occurred hull sailboats were being used to exploit a particular marketable species of fish. Second, the fishing ports from which
hull sailboats operated were located near to and in communication with
large urban markets. Third, changes from log rafts to hull sailboats
relate directly to the distance from the source of jangada wood. In every
case the distance from the source of logs used in the manufacture of
rafts was so great that the cost of rafts had increased to a degree that
prohibited their purchase by peasant fishermen.

It is important to note here that the presence of jangada wood alone
does not account for the spread of raft fishing. While the few jangadas
found in southern Bahia state are in one of the only remaining areas
where *pau de jangada* is available, the predominant fishing technique
in that region is canoe and net fishing. Moreover, few jangadas are
found in the Amazon region, which has now become one of the chief
sources of supply of the logs used in their construction. It is far more
probable that the failure to use rafts in large numbers in these areas
accounts for the continued availability of jangada wood there.

At the same time, the persistence of raft fishing in Alagoas is undoubtedly related to the availability of jangada wood in that state.

While a supply of logs is available from the Amazon, the cost of transportation prohibits its purchase by peasant fishermen in the Northeast. The same log that currently costs $4 in Alagoas sells for over $8 in Ceará and up to $12 in Paraiba state. The fact that the state of Alagoas still boasts a supply of jangada wood despite the large number of rafts that are concentrated in the region is undoubtedly related to the law of 1798 that placed all marine woods in the area under reserve for the Portuguese Royal Navy. (We will return to this point in the next chapter.) It is also apparent that the wood resources in Alagoas will disappear soon, making a change in the traditional raft fishing economy inevitable. *Pau de jangada* is part of a secondary forest which has a maximum life span of 150 to 200 years (Richards 1957:297–99), and the original cover in the Northeast has long since been cleared (James 1959:424). Even calculating on the basis of a 200-year life span with minimal exploitation of the resource, the supply of logs will end soon. At that time fishermen will be forced to accept new boat types as they have been in most other areas in Brazil.

THE HISTORY OF RAFT FISHING

The raft fishing industry in Northeast Brazil has been and continues to be a part economy with roots deep in the pre-Columbian past. Since the coming of the European to the New World raft fishing has become an integral part of a national economic system which includes a wide variety of other peasant types (Siegel 1955:401 *et passim*, Oberg 1965:1425).[3] The importance of the industry to the nation is reflected in federal legislation effected through government agencies and through a national fishermen's guild. The peasant fisherman has always contributed a supply of food to the plantation hinterland and to urban zones, and the man in power has always acted in the interest of maintaining that supply.

Before the Portuguese came, coastal Indians cooperated in the exploitation of the total ecological sphere available to them. The Portuguese subsequently imposed a structured set of social alignments and transformed these subsistence economies into commodity producers for people engaged in the production of commercial export crops. The early travel literature on Brazil is full of reports of plantation owners sending Indians, and later Africans, out to fish on rafts (Verdonck 1630:223, Brandão n.d.:231, Soarès de Souza 1587:347, Almeida Prado 1941:249). Since legislation dictated where fishing was to be done, where fish were to be sold, and at what price (Documentos históricos 1625:6, 36; Freyre 1963:126), it is likely that a system of peonage—and not slavery—prevailed in the fishing economy.[4]

Where European powers extended their political, economic, and social control in colonial times, local producers expanded their purely subsistence activities and took on a new role as producers for the nation and consumers of the nation's products. The allocation of personnel to particular economic roles, whether as commodity producers or as part of the labor force, which was formerly based on mutual dependence, now came to be based on structured power relationships (Furtado 1963:132, Wolf 1966:11). With this transformation, the subsistence producer entered the money economy. It is essential to note, however, that in his role as commodity producer or laborer, the peasant has remained largely marginal to the national economy, and his role as a subsistence producer has hardly changed. He stands on the very margin of a monetary system in which the slightest inflationary fluxes or recession in the national economy can suddenly thrust him back to a subsistence level (Furtado 1963:70–71, 144). At the same time, the establishment of a market economy based on money exchange requires his participation, no matter how minimal, if he is to enjoy the barest necessities: that is, the peasant must buy at least some of his food and most of his clothing and household supplies at the local market. It is in this sense that peasant economies can be treated as traditional aspects of larger economic systems. The peasant does not participate fully, and certainly not directly, in the advances that take place in the nation at large. On the contrary, even the new technologies introduced by the Europeans into the peasant sector of the economy in the past were oriented largely toward fulfilling their own consumption needs.

Historically, there has been reason to limit the introduction of techniques which might permit the accumulation of wealth and status by fishermen and by entrepreneurs residing on privately owned plantation lands.[5] Primitive technology precluded the possibility of raft fishermen gaining control over resources at sea and sharply curtailed their earning power. Since the logs for constructing rafts had to be obtained from plantation lands, fishermen were always under the control of the planters. On land fishermen were subject to further restrictions. Religious brotherhoods and, later, fishermen's guilds directed the course of all fishing activities. Raft fishing, by virtue of its not allowing for differences in the accumulation of individual wealth, was permitted to continue as long as it served as an adequate producer of fish for hungry landowners and slaves.

Despite the fishermen's familiarity with a variety of fishing techniques, the fishing industry in Northeast Brazil has maintained an essentially traditional character. This is so because the indigenous raft fishing technology encountered by the Portuguese has proven adequate up to now for both producers and consumers. Limited changes have occurred, but large-scale reorganization has not yet come. The changes that the raft fishing economy has undergone have been limited in extent and have done little to alter the basic economic organization of fishing communities. Some broader changes have, nevertheless, been occurring slowly, accompanied by an entirely new set of economic relationships and, particularly, by a systematic redistribution of wealth, which often works to the disadvantage of the peasant fishermen. All of these changes appear to be the result of two sets of variables. The first represent ecological variations and adaptations easily accepted by small independent producers. The second are large-scale technological changes resulting from enterpreneurial control over strategic land resources, which allows the imposition of new techniques on dependent fishermen.

Among the first type of changes we can include the variations in the size of rafts and the additional accoutrements, such as the lateen sail and salting platforms introduced by the Portuguese.[6] The rafts were originally quite small and were fished by one man near the shore (Camara Cascudo 1957b:11). It is not unlikely that sea voyages began with the introduction of the lateen sail, thus opening up new fishing grounds further offshore. These were small-scale adaptive changes over a period of time that were easily woven into the cultural repertoire of individual fishermen without widespread disruption in the productive unit.

On the other hand, large-scale technological changes, such as the introduction of hull sailboats or nets by entrepreneurs with a profit motive, may significantly alter the fishing pattern. These are often accompanied by a new set of social relationships based on the exploitation of natural resources by a human labor pool, which reduces the independent producer to a kind of sharecropper. When such reorganization in the productive unit results in a profit loss to independent producers, it is met with considerable resistance (Fraser 1960). Whether this resistance is successful or not depends, in the main, on the other choices open to the peasant producer.

Economic organization within the community itself has always been premised on the replacement of traditional equipment rather than on innovation. This is not because raft fishermen do not desire change, but because, with limited marketing facilities in most areas and the inability to control prices, they do not realize any immediate economic advantage in change. Moreover, the rise of an effective middleman is prevented by familial obligations, which constantly cause the number of fish hawkers to multiply. Indeed, only when entrepreneurs with outside capitalization have invested in the fishing industry have large-scale technological changes from rafts to hull sailboats been effected. Such changes have always been stimulated by new market possibilities, and in order to be successful they require that fishermen abandon independent production on their own log rafts in favor of fishing as members of a crew.

From the point of view of the peasant producer, independent production may well be more remunerative than fishing as a member of a crew on someone else's boat. The low productive capacity among raft fishermen in Northeast Brazil undoubtedly can be attributed to the primitive technology still used in that region. The technology persists because it is part of a consistently adaptive pattern that has not yet been stimulated to change. Raft fishermen yield to change when they are faced either with the promise of immediate economic gain or with an inability to maintain their traditional fishing patterns owing to the rising prices of logs. In the latter case they are encouraged to seek employment as crew members on hull sailboats belonging to enterpreneurs who wish to take advantage of a consumer market by utilizing an inexpensive labor pool. While such changes offer obvious advantages to the owner of the craft, they do not always prove beneficial to the peasant fisherman. In cases where resources still permit peasant fishermen to construct their own log rafts and continue as independent producers, it is to their best personal advantage to reject changes in boat type.

Often, however, the prohibitive price of logs results in the grouping of formerly independent fishermen on commercial fishing vessels. Fishermen who are unable to replace even their small rafts sail on larger boats, from which they exploit high-quality species of fish for urban markets. They contribute a significant share of the catch to a nonfishing owner. In all such cases, there is a marked concentration in the patterns of ownership and reduction in the number of middlemen, with a diminishing reliance on kin ties in the distribution of fish.

Two examples of such changes are evident in the exploitation of *albacora* (*Thunnus atlanticus*), or albacore, off the coast of Rio Grande do Norte, and in the rock lobster fishing industry in the state of Ceará. In the first example, log rafts began to be replaced by the far more expensive plank rafts and by hull sailboats some forty years ago (Cruz e Paiva 1964:2, Camara Cascudo 1957a:84). The fishermen are supplied with all equipment in exchange for half of the catch.[7] The lobster fishing companies, by contrast, pay the fishermen a monthly salary, equivalent to the minimum salary in the region, but the company keeps the whole catch. In the community of Majorlândia, Ceará, the entire fleet of twenty-four rafts is owned by a single company. It is interesting that in Ceará the fishermen's guild is the most active in Northeast Brazil and that the lobster companies pay all of the dues and taxes required of the fishermen (Paiva 1959:41). In this way, they gain control over the guild and, thereby, over the fishermen's source of credit.

While this arrangement has enabled enterpreneurs to employ an available labor force effectively in the exploitation of a marketable commodity, it has proven detrimental to the fishermen, themselves, in the long run. The lobster fishing companies are now confronted with the very serious problem of the overexploitation of resources. This accounts for the recent cessation of operations in the states of Rio Grande do Norte and Paraiba. In one community, I arrived in time to see the rafts and lobster traps being loaded on trucks. The manager of the company, who was supervising the operation, explained that diminishing returns were forcing the company to withdraw to the north. The effects on the local fishermen were disastrous since the company withdrawal left them without their own individual means of production.

In the absence of an equitable share system independent production proves far more profitable than fishing on someone else's craft. Often independent production can lead to the rejection of new techniques, even though such a rejection means that a general increase in over-all production may be sacrificed. What we must take into account is not the total daily production of a number of vessels, but the production of individual vessels counted over longer periods of time and the way in which the catch is divided among the fishermen.

The log raft, which now appears inadequate as an instrument of production, was once held in such high esteem that Brazilian entrepreneurs made several attempts to introduce them into the northern state of Maranhão in the early nineteenth century (Alves Camara 1888:9). It is interesting, and indeed revealing, to note that one account of the failure of raft fishing to take hold in this region blames the "irrational behavior of indolent fishermen," despite evidence that clearly points to ecological and economic reasons for the failure (*Ibid.*, 27).

In 1868, two jangadas were sent from the northeast state of Ceará to the northern state of Maranhão, each with a crew of three men who were under individual contract to the owner at a monthly wage (*Ibid.*, 28). The rafts opened up new fishing grounds hitherto unreached by canoes, which traditionally ply the brackish waters of the Amazon region; but they did so at great cost to the crew members. The rafts had to sail some thirty hours to reach the fishing grounds, sometimes failing to arrive there because of insufficient winds. Furthermore, especially strong currents kept hooks and line afloat in spite of a two-pound weight. Although first-class commercial species of fish that had never before been seen in the markets of Maranhão were caught in abundance, these were attacked by sharks as soon as they were hooked, and within a half hour the rafts were fully encircled by blood (*Ibid.*, 29). Despite these difficulties, the owner of the rafts realized a considerable profit; at times the profit per fishing expedition exceeded the monthly wage of each crew member. Yet the individual crew members received no additional compensation for their extra labors, and they eventually abandoned the rafts. Although their contracts afforded them return passage to their native state, they chose to remain and fish for themselves on the canoes common to the region (*Ibid.*, 30).

The same kind of rational behavior led to the rejection of hull sailboats by the raft fishermen of Coqueiral. As in the case cited above, an understanding of the rejection of innovations depends upon the study of complex relationships in a complex setting and not upon the analysis of individual motivations. Similarly, it would be wrong to attribute the maintenance of a traditional economic system merely to an inherent cultural conservatism on the part of peasants. As the following pages will show, the failure of technological innovation to take hold among the raft fishermen of Coqueiral can be attributed to a lack of inducement to change and to possible economic benefits. The obstacles to change in Coqueiral are not so much psychological or cognitive as they are economic and social.

The Community: Coqueiral

THE SETTING

COQUEIRAL is a coastal community of 852 people located at 10.4° south latitude and 37.8° west longitude in the county of Guaiamu in the state of Alagoas, in Northeast Brazil (see Map I). A primary feature of the locale is the large, crescent-shaped bay which opens to the southwest. The village is situated at the northeast extremity of this bay, providing a safe harbor for ships.[1] The southwest corner of the bay, at the mouth of the Guaiamu River, is the site of another village, Baxias, which specializes in canoe and net fishing. At the easternmost tip of the bay, due east of the village of Coqueiral, a lighthouse sends a beam fourteen miles out to sea to warn ships of the low-lying reefs that dot the area. A sandstone reef juts out from the bottom of the high sand dune upon which the lighthouse sits. At high tide, it forms a series of shallow pools into which resident fishermen cast conical hand nets; summer visitors swim in these same pools. From the shore end of this reef an open beach, pounded by heavy surf, runs due north for several miles. The harbor is protected by two outer reefs, one of which lies some five miles out and the other, approximately ten miles from shore. In addition to entrances at the extreme north and south ends, three major breaks in these reefs provide access to the harbor for small boats.

HISTORY

Coqueiral has a history of contact with the outside world by sea.[2] A series of maritime adventures began early in the sixteenth century when French frigates came to trade for dyewoods with the Caeté Indians, who inhabited this section of the coast.[3] The Caeté, a sub-

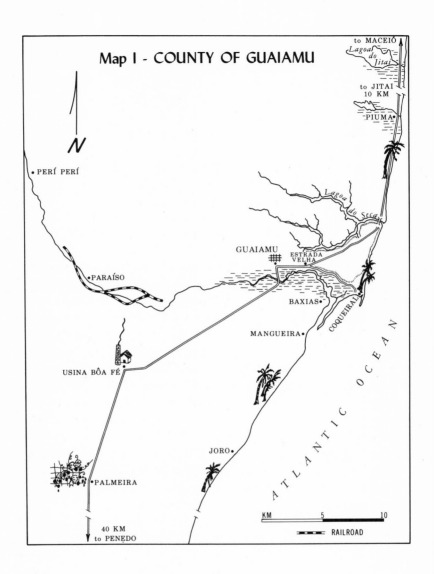

Map I - COUNTY OF GUAIAMU

N

to MACEIÓ
Lagoa do Jitai

to JITAI
10 KM

PIUMA•

• PERÍ PERÍ

Lagoa do Seca

GUAIAMU
ESTRADA
VELHA

•PARAÍSO

BAXIAS•

COQUEIRAL

MANGUEIRA•

ATLANTIC OCEAN

USINA BÔA FÉ

JORO•

•PALMEIRA

KM   5   10

40 KM
to PENEDO

RAILROAD

division of the coastal Tupinambá tribe, farmed and fished on the small rafts which have prevailed to the present day (Soares de Souza 1938:32). In 1556, the first Bishop of Brazil, Dom Pedro Fernandes Sardinha, was shipwrecked on the Dom Rodrigues rocks to the southeast of Coqueiral and came ashore at the village. He promptly was taken prisoner by the Caeté and later eaten. As a result of this incident, there was a deliberate campaign the following year to eradicate the Caeté. Subsequently the village was inhabited by pacified Indians of the Potiguar tribe from the north and by a few Portuguese settlers. These villagers lived by fishing, subsistence farming, and the continued exploitation of *pau-brasil* (dyewood) (Indicador Geral 1902:197–98).

For the remainder of the sixteenth and seventeenth centuries the area served as a commodity producer for the sugar cane planters around the provincial capital of Olinda, in the present-day state of Pernambuco (Almeida Prado 1941:445–46, Correia de Andrade 1959:40).[4] The area took on initial importance from the raising of cattle (Correia de Andrade 1959:50). When sugar was planted in the valley of Guaiamu in the eighteenth century, Coqueiral became a summer playground for the local planters and a port for the shipment of sugar and salt to the north. The goods were transported on small, locally built cargo carriers called *bacaças*.[5] The community also became a source of food and fuel for the hinterland, supplying fish, mollusks, and wood from the mangrove swamp to the sugar plantations.

The state of Alagoas came under such rapid exploitation that in 1798 the rich forest resources were put under reserve for the Portuguese Royal Navy. Land use in the southern counties was strictly limited to arid areas where the valuable hardwoods did not grow.[6] As a result, the population of the coastal area grew rapidly. The heavily furrowed plots, now abandoned on the tableland above Coqueiral, indicate that the land was farmed intensively. Archaeological evidence also points to widespread settlement in the immediate area.[7]

In 1871, Coqueiral boasted sixty tile-roofed houses and two *sobrados* (mansions), suggesting the probable existence of a number of wattle-and-daub dwellings as well. At this time, a railroad from the Alagoan hinterland to the port of Coqueiral was planned to facilitate the

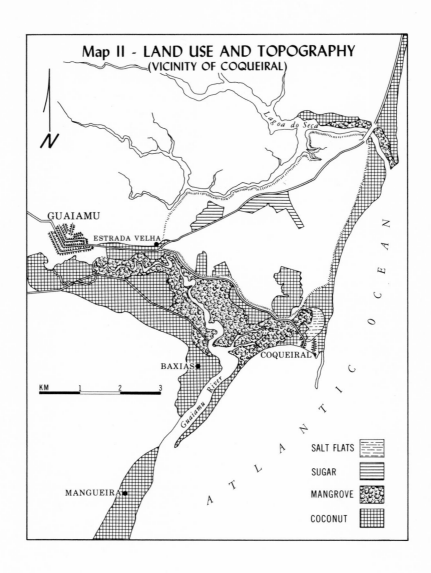

Map II - LAND USE AND TOPOGRAPHY
(VICINITY OF COQUEIRAL)

N

Lagoa do Seca

GUAIAMU

ESTRADA VELHA

COQUEIRAL

BAXIAS

KM   1   2   3

Guaiamu River

MANGUEIRA

ATLANTIC OCEAN

SALT FLATS
SUGAR
MANGROVE
COCONUT

shipment of processed sugar to the coast (Espindola 1871:236–37, Correia de Andrade 1959:45). Although the present-day capital of Maceió was to become the railroad terminal, the port at Coqueiral remained quite active into the early twentieth century. The geographer Costa (1901:109) reports that at the turn of the century the village was made up of about three hundred buildings, inhabited by approximately a thousand people who were primarily maritime workers and their families. There is no indication that this count included fishermen, although the relatively small movement of cargo vessels, numbering only a few a week, would suggest that the majority of "maritime workers" were probably fishermen.

Shipping activity increased in the 1920's when the valley's sugar mill was built, and salt production reached its peak in the village. In the 1930's, however, the salt flats were abandoned when federal quotas were taken away. About this time, the cattle remaining in the immediate coastal area were moved west, to the far side of the valley. The improvement of roads, which facilitated the shipping of sugar by land, rendered the port of Coqueiral useless, and the villagers reverted to primarily subsistence work. In 1965, the only activity in the harbor at Coqueiral was fishing, and the exploitation of land resources was greatly curtailed.

TOPOGRAPHY AND LAND USE

The topography of the narrow coastal plain imposes strict limitations on land use around Coqueiral (see Map II). Directly behind the houses on the west side of the village lies a mangrove swamp that bounds the Guaiamu River to the place where it empties into the sea some three miles below Coqueiral. The river is salty from the action of the tides, and is navigable as far as the city of Guaiamu. The village of Baxias is located just across from the swamp on the other side of the river.

The mangrove swamp serves the entire population of both villages as an important source of fuel and mollusks, and as a free feeding ground for pigs. The residents of the village of Estrada Velha, which is situated midway between Coqueiral and Guaiamu, the county seat, make their living almost exclusively from the sale of crabs, caught in

abundance in the muddy banks of the swamp. A woman from Coqueiral planted some fifty coconut palms in a clearing in the swamp,
and one of the retired fishermen blocked out a small subsistence plot
on a raised island in the middle of the swamp. The mangrove root
is used for the weaving of baskets for fish and bait, and certain mangrove leaves are used to treat fishing line. The river itself is the primary
source of bait, without which the fishing economy could not be successfully carried out in the winter.

Coqueiral is bounded on the north by the abandoned salt flats,
which give way to a tableland that rises sharply some 150 meters and
extends about six kilometers inland to where the valley of Guaiamu
itself begins. This tableland measures approximately one square league
(1 league = 6,000 meters). It was bequeathed to the Catholic Church
in 1834. Since that time the land has been parcelled out to individual
renters at Cr$50 ($.03) per *tarefa* (3,052 square meters per *tarefa*)
per year. Many of the holdings have been rented by the same family
for generations. As early as 1871, the township of Guaiamu was reported to have been a refuge for migrants from the drought-parched
region of the Northeast and a source of supply of manioc, beans, corn
oil, salt, and even fruits for the state capital (Espindola 1871:236–37).

The tableland, or *chã*, represents the total land area for farming
available to the residents of Coqueiral, Guaiamu, and Estrada Velha,
the village located between the coast and the county capital. Almost
all of the 3,600 hectares (10,000 square meters per hectare), or 11,800
tarefas available are located on the tableland that stretches behind the
village from the Guaiamu River to Lagôa Sêca, a small settlement
situated on a lagoon of the same name. The soils of the tableland are a
clay and sandy-clay mixture of fluvial and marine sediments (Maio
1962:40–41 and Domingues 1962:177), which are not considered very
good for agriculture (James 1959:412).

It has been estimated that in order for a subsistence farmer to
obtain good crops from 5 hectares of poor land under an adequate
system of land rotation, he would need a total of 80 to 105 hectares
at his disposal (Oberg 1965:1425).[8] Given the population pressures
on the available land and the differential access to the land, which is
controlled in the county capital, the villagers of Coqueiral do not
enjoy even the minimal conditions described. The total land area

now available to well over one thousand families in the Guaiamu coastal area, if divided up to meet such "good crop" estimates, would yield only forty-five *roças*, or subsistence farms. Together, the villagers of Coqueiral and Estrada Velha hold many more than this number of individual farm sites, with the result that the diminished size of their plots makes even subsistence agriculture in the immediate area relatively ineffectual.

The largest single holding on the tableland is five hundred *tarefas*. It is held by a family who reside in the county capital and is completely planted in coconut palms. Less than five hundred *tarefas* are held by all of the villagers of Coqueiral. The largest single holding among them is approximately one hundred *tarefas*, planted in coconuts. Another holding of fifty and one of forty *tarefas* also are planted in coconuts. About thirty village households rent plots of under ten *tarefas* each, the average being approximately two *tarefas* per agricultural household.

Large holdings, like the five hundred *tarefas* held by one man in Guaiamu, are rented year after year by the same family, and the right to inherit such holdings is recognized by the Church. The small plots of land are divided among individual peasant farmers, who pay rent only on that portion of the land which they are farming at the moment. A good portion of uncultivated land thereby reverts to the Church each year and lies fallow until it is rented again.

Few of the fishermen in Coqueiral engage in any kind of agricultural activity, although members of their kindred do. Most fishermen choose to retain their small tableland plots for the seasonal yield of one or two fruit trees, primarily mango and cashew, which provide a welcome supplement to a low calorie diet. It is interesting that fishermen claim they would not be agriculturalists under any circumstances because their personalities simply will not allow it. It is more probable, however, that the extensive roots of the coconut palms and the shade from the mango trees inhibit planting that might otherwise be done in the area.

It is difficult to determine if years of heavy planting have so thoroughly leached the soils that only coconut palms will flourish, or if the planting of coconut renders the land useless for other types of cultivation. Whatever the case, the majority of smaller plots of one to four *tarefas* are not farmed, but are held for the few fruit trees they bear. A common complaint among the villagers is that it does not pay to plant a crop for animals owned by someone else to destroy. Yet, there is evidence to indicate that the raising of sheep, goats, and pigs that feed freely on the tableland may be of more economic importance to the community than the fencing in of tiny plots for the cultivation of subsistence crops.

The primary agricultural activity in the immediate area of Coqueiral is coconut planting. While coconuts represent a lifelong investment of some worth, offering six harvests per annum, the five to seven years necessary for a tree to bear its first marketable crop makes coconut planting commercially unfeasible for the small farmer. Moreover, since a four- to nine-meter space is required between each tree, commercial coconut groves are found on rather large landholdings. While extensive areas both along the beach and on the tableland are given over to groves, only thirty-five villagers have coconut crops of any commercial value. Some groves were inherited and thus are owned; others are planted on land rented from the Church. Trees planted along the beach and in the mangrove swamp actually grow on marine lands belonging to the public domain. Possession of coconut groves in the public domain does not give their owner rights over the land, but the trees themselves have high commercial value. A full-grown tree averages twenty coconuts per harvest. Saplings sell for Cr$5,000–Cr$6,000 ($2.50–$3.50).[9] The dried and husked coconuts themselves sell for Cr$35,000–Cr$50,000 ($20–$27) per thousand. In sharp contrast, a coconut harvester receives Cr$30 (under $.02) for each tree climbed, and a husker earns Cr$250 ($.13) per hundred coconuts. All of the coconuts grown around Coqueiral are sold to truckers from the South through a dealer who lives in the county seat.

The largest single planter in Coqueiral owns approximately twelve hundred trees, not all of them productive. In 1965 one harvest alone yielded some eleven thousand coconuts. This brings his monthly income to nearly four times that of the owner of the largest raft in the village. The same man rents the largest piece of land on the *chā* and owns several rafts and nets. Two other villagers own one thousand trees apiece. In addition, there are at least four owners with approximately five hundred trees apiece, seven owners with around one hun-

Coconut harvester at work in Coqueiral

dred coconut palms, and seven others with about fifty. The remaining
fourteen commercial producers have approximately ten coconut trees
each. The majority of villagers in Coqueiral own one or two trees at
most and use the fruits only for home consumption. While one or
two coconut palms are planted in almost every backyard, they often
belong to one of the commercial planters, and not to the household.

ECONOMIC ORGANIZATION IN THE COUNTY (MUNICIPIO)[10]

The agricultural wealth in the county of Guaiamu is based on sugar
cane production and refining, which is concentrated in the center of
the valley. Fifteen thousand of the valley's forty thousand hectares
are owned by the sugar mill, the Usina Bôa Fé, which is located fifteen
kilometers from the county seat and twenty-one kilometers from
Coqueiral along the same road (see Map I). Of the six to ten thousand
hectares cultivated annually, some five thousand belong to the sugar
mill. Of the two hundred thousand tons of sugar cane harvested in
1965, one hundred thirty thousand tons were produced on lands owned
outright by the Usina. The remainder was purchased from a number of
small producers in the valley. The mill itself exported some three
hundred thousand sacks of sugar in 1965.

Despite the size of the mill operation, which is the third largest in
the state of Alagoas, the opportunity for wage work within the county
is limited. Only six of the 300 factory workers in the Usina are from
Coqueiral: four of them are sons of local coconut planters, and two
others were hired ostensibly for their skill on the Usina's soccer team.
Aside from a small commercial still for the production of sugar cane
rum, there is one other industrial activity in the county, also based on
agriculture.[11] This is the production of *maracujá* fruit juice and jelly at
the internationally financed agricultural colony of Palmeira, located
in a neighboring valley at the southwestern boundary of the county.
None of the villagers from Coqueiral were working in Palmeira in
1965.

The extreme limitations on land use around Coqueiral and the lack
of opportunity for wage work in the county as a whole have helped
to make fishing the predominant economic activity in the village. The
importance of the fishing industry in Coqueiral is indicated by the

fact that 111 out of 193 adults males earn their principal livelihood from some aspect of the fishing economy. Of these, eighty-five men are engaged in fishing as their primary activity. Some twelve retired fishermen receive monthly pensions of Cr$26,000 ($14) from the Maritime Institute. Although 10% of the pensioners' income is spent on transportation to and from the state capital, where pensions are paid out, retirement pay constitutes one of the most steady sources of income in the village. Three more men, one a resident of the county capital, receive monthly salaries of Cr$77,000 ($42) for the performance of bureaucratic duties connected with the fishing industry. Another obtains his principal source of income from a percentage of the taxes taken from all sales of fish. Ten men and eleven women are also self-employed as fish hawkers. The overwhelming majority of women, 214 out of 276, earn their living from the manufacture of straw baskets. The disproportionate number of females in relation to adult males may be explained in part by the inclusion in the tally of children who help their mothers with the basketmaking, and in part by the differential rate of emigration of males from the village. The entire range of occupational distribution among the villagers is listed according to their principal source of income in Table 1.*

TABLE 1. OCCUPATIONAL DISTRIBUTION OF MALES AND
FEMALES IN COQUEIRAL

MALES		FEMALES	
Occupation	*Number*	*Occupation*	*Number*
Fishermen	85	Basketmakers	214
Retired fishermen	12	Lacemakers	2
Fish hawkers	10	Seamstresses	6
Agriculturalists	38	Fish hawkers	11
Coconut workers	16	Teachers	2
Bureaucrats	4	Other	41
Carpenters	4		
Wage laborers	15		
Other	9		
Total	193		276 = 469

* All demographic and economic data were collected as part of a general household census and survey conducted in July and August 1965.

Out of a total of 198 households in 1965, 38 were headed by women who earned their living from the manufacture of straw baskets. Of the remaining 160 households, 102 earn their principal source of income from the fishing economy, either directly, as fishermen and middlemen, or indirectly, as pensioners and public functionaries. The occupational distribution of the heads of households is also evidence of the importance of fishing in the over-all life of the village.

TABLE 2. OCCUPATIONAL DISTRIBUTION OF HEADS
OF HOUSEHOLDS IN COQUEIRAL

Fishing	65
Fishing and fish hawking	3
Fish hawking	18
Pensioners	12
Public functionaries	4
Agriculture	28
Basketry	38
Other	30
Total households	198

MIGRATION

The limited agricultural resources of Coqueiral would not seem to encourage immigration. Yet, the open resources of the sea are slightly more attractive. Approximately 38% of the present male and over 40% of the present female heads of households were born outside of the village. Fifty per cent of the immigrant males and 42% of the immigrant females were born within the country itself. The remainder came from the drought-ridden backlands, where they had no way to sustain themselves. In Coqueiral, they were willing to take up any work that would provide them with food and clothing. Three out of five of the males born outside of the village took up fishing or some sort of occasional wage labor for a living. The remainder blocked out small subsistence plots. A large number of people continue to live along the banks of the Guaiamu River in the neighboring village of Estrada Velha, making their livelihood by collecting crabs in the mangrove swamp.

The fishing economy can absorb only a limited number of people before overfishing or the glutting of the market become serious problems. There has been a steady stream of emigration, which has probably increased in size since the 1920's. At that time the abandonment of the salt flats and the closing of the port to commercial traffic significantly reduced the number of wage-work opportunities in the village. An examination of data gathered from the present generation of household heads indicates that 162 of their brothers and sons and 97 of their sisters and daughters have left the village. These figures represent 78% of the present adult male and 35% of the present adult female population. The far larger emigration of men reflects the limited possibilities for employment in the fishing industry, as opposed to the greater elasticity of the straw basket industry, which can absorb female personnel. Boys and girls up to fifteen years old tend to leave Coqueiral at the same general rate. Although the rate increases greatly between fifteen and twenty-five years of age for both sexes, the proportion of male emigrants in this age group is almost double that for females. From twenty-five to thirty years of age the rate of emigration drops by approximately half for both sexes, and after thirty years of age it tends to decline steadily as the resident population of the village stabilizes. The rate of emigration of males and females from the village is shown in Table 3.

TABLE 3. EMIGRATION FROM COQUEIRAL OF MALES AND FEMALES
WITH RELATIVES REMAINING IN THE VILLAGE

AGE	MALE	FEMALE
5–9	5	1
10–14	7	6
15–19	52	25
20–24	45	32
25–29	25	13
30–34	9	8
35–39	4	4
40–44	11	6
45–49	2	
50–	2	2
Total	162	97

Table 4. Emigration from Coqueiral of Males with Relatives Remaining in the Village

AGE UPON LEAVING	MARITAL STATUS		OCCUPATION ON LEAVING					DESTINATION						OCCUPATION ON ARRIVAL					
	Single	Married	Fishing	Agriculture	Student	Coconut Worker	Wage Labor	Corumpe	Maceió	Usina	Aracajú	Hinterland	Rio-São Paulo-Recife	Laborer	Commerce	Agriculture	Fishing	Military	Student
5–9	5	.	.	.	5	.	.	.	5	.	.	.	.	2	2	.	1	.	1
10–14	8	.	1	.	7	.	.	3	3	1	1	1	2	.	4	.	8	.	3
15–19	50	2	19	4	20	6	3	3	12	3	13	3	19	18	7	11	8	5	3
20–24	38	7	17	8	14	2	4	5	14	1	3	4	18	20	2	11	8	3	1
25–29	10	15	19	4	.	1	1	4	8	1	3	4	5	10	.	9	6	.	.
30–34	3	6	8	.	.	.	.	.	7	.	2	.	.	.	1	.	8	.	.
35–39	.	4	1	3	.	1	.	1	1	.	1	.	1	1	1	1	1	.	.
40–44	4	7	5	2	.	3	1	1	3	.	3	1	3	5	1	1	4	.	.
45–49	.	2	.	.	.	.	2	.	.	.	1	.	1	1	.	1	.	.	.
50–	.	2	.	2	.	.	.	.	.	.	2	.	.	.	.	2	.	.	.

Almost 70% of the male emigrants were single and over 40% were fishermen at the time they left the village. Some 28% went to the metropolitan centers of Recife (Pernambuco), Rio de Janeiro, and São Paulo. Another 20% continued to live in or near the county and are engaged in agricultural work. Approximately 50% of the émigrés went to the state capital of Maceió and the nearby city of Aracajú, capital of the state of Sergipe. About 37% of the emigrants entered the urban labor pool. Another 20% went into agricultural work, many as coconut harvesters and huskers on the extensive plantations around Aracajú. Only 20% continued to fish after leaving the village. The rest entered commerce, continued their studies, or joined the military in the city (see Table 4).

While the emigrants to Rio de Janeiro, São Paulo, and Recife are less likely to return to Coqueiral, many who go to Maceió and Aracajú to fish do come back. Approximately 43% of the resident male population of Coqueiral has worked outside of the village at some point. Some 54% of these are fishermen who came back with capital to invest in rafts. The remainder tend to stay away, since there is no land to return to, and the highly perishable fishing equipment is not a very valuable inheritance. Only 20% of those who migrate and return to the village enter agriculture.

Since neither the sugar mill nor the Palmeira colony uses migrant labor at harvest time, there is almost no seasonal migration for work. Five men did go to Aracajú to fish in the summer of 1965, but they were expected to return the following winter, when passage to and from the Port at Aracajú becomes too dangerous for small fishing vessels.[12]

COMMUNICATION

Direct communications between coastal villages are minimal, save for traffic along the beach to and from the coconut plantations during harvest time or for an occasional social visit. Women formerly did their wash in a fresh-water spring in Lagôa Sêca, but are now forbidden to use the privately-owned font. Limited communication with the outside world is established through an occasional sailboat from Maceió or Aracajú which takes refuge in the harbor during a storm. And a few

canoes come down the Guaiamu River from Estrada Velha to set
beach seines at its mouth. The main lines of communication from
Coqueiral follow along a well-traveled dirt road which leads some
seven kilometers from the village inland to the county seat. Although
there is no public transportation to Coqueiral, several private cars
make the trip from Guaiamu almost daily, either in search of fresh fish
or to use the beach. The majority of travelers to and from the county
seat, however, are villagers who make the trip on foot or on mule back.

It is in Guaiamu that almost all of the political and bureaucratic
functions of the county are carried out. One goes there to register
births and to bury the dead. On rare occasions a mass is celebrated in
the church in Coqueiral, but for the most part, the priest remains in
Guaiamu or travels among the many chapels in the hinterland, where
sugar cane grows. A primary school functions most of the time in the
village, when the teachers can come from Guaiamu. Another primary
school is maintained in Coqueiral by the local branch of the national
fishermen's guild, for the children of fishermen.

The entire economy of Coqueiral is linked to outside markets. In
addition to the regular sale of coconuts and straw baskets, fish must be
sold daily in Guaiamu, and some at the weekly markets at the sugar
mill and at the Palmeira colony. There is also a large demand for
consumer goods in the village. Every Saturday morning the road to
Guaiamu is crowded with villagers who walk back and forth to the
weekly market. Seventy-five was the smallest number of households
represented at the Guaiamu market one rainy winter day when approximately Cr$225,000 ($125) was spent on consumer items. Most
of the small inventory in Coqueiral's seven small general stores, or
shops, also is bought at the Saturday fair. These stores are supplemented by a chain of traders who come to the village to sell fruits,
biscuits, crackers, and the sugar cane rum (cachaça) that is brewed in
the western part of the valley. A bread man, who lives in Coqueiral,
represents a bakery in the county seat, where he makes his purchases
every second day. Almost none of the agricultural produce grown by
the villagers on the tableland makes its way to the Saturday fair
in Guaiamu. Whatever small surplus is left over usually is sold in the
cultivator's house in the village, and advertised by a sample in the
window.

Coqueiral is, therefore, closely tied to the outside world. The village is dependent on the county and the nation at large, and capital is drawn off almost daily for a variety of goods and services which cannot be provided by the villagers. Increases in the price of fish have not kept pace with rampant inflation as a result of the price ceilings imposed by the mayor and the president of the local fishermen's guild. This situation appears in sharp contrast to the one described by Kottak (1966:200 *et passim*) in which the price of fish in Arembepe has risen faster than the cost of boats. The differential effects of inflation in Arembepe, where price controls are not rigidly imposed, enable fishermen to buy their own vessels. In Coqueiral, as we shall see, the fishermen's expenditures often outweigh his income. Overall, the drain on capital exceeds the income derived from commodities that are produced in Coqueiral, and the villagers have little liquid capital at their disposal. While they are able to accumulate enough money to replace their rafts, there is almost no capital available for experimentation with new fishing equipment.

[III]

Social Structure and the Peasant Economy

THE ACCUMULATION of wealth in the county of Guaiamu is derived not from fishing but from agriculture. The structure of the fishing economy in Coqueiral is affected by the system of stratification in the county. A social hierarchy based on outside sources of political power and wealth operates in both the systems of production and distribution, and the sources of credit are carefully controlled. The large-scale sugar planters, and particularly the owners of the mill, are at the top of the social hierarchy. They exercise economic and political hegemony over the valley as a whole. At the next level, there is a group of smaller landowners and lesser bureaucrats, professional men, and tradesmen who reside in the county seat. Below them are the coconut planters resident in Coqueiral and, at the bottom, the bulk of the villagers. Power in the village is wielded through bureaucratic positions connected to the fishing industry and obtained through political patronage.

A landowning elite, which was formerly resident in the village, moved away when cattle raising and salt production ceased. They have been replaced by local "bigwigs" who have come to occupy a position of power within the village.[1] "Os grandes do lugar" (the big men of the place), as they are called by the fishermen, have filled the vacuum left by the traditional local patrão. Born in the village of lower-class families, they actually stand just above the peasant fishermen in status, although, for the most part, they have managed to earn a better living than the fishermen, and they maintain a standard of living slightly above the norm. As a group, these bigwigs bear closer resemblance to the town-type subculture of the county seat than they do to the local peasant subculture (Wagley and Harris 1955:438). In Coqueiral they are, so to speak, the "biggest frogs in the pond."

Although they attempt to emulate the upper-class townsmen, the

A street in the village

local bigwigs have highly limited social mobility. Like the peasant whom they tend to disdain, they, too, are continually in debt, to the sugar planters for their land or to the tradesmen in the city, as a result of overextended patterns of consumption. These debts tie them to the village. While they themselves cannot afford to move out, the bigwigs do try to send their children away to study, either to the county seat or state capital, where they live with relatives who belong to the urban proletariat. In certain respects, the fishermen have a higher degree of spatial mobility since their limited number of debts and small stock of worldly goods do not anchor them to the community.

The status of the local bigwigs is largely dependent on their identification with the traditional power structure in the county at large. It is through such identification that they exert a tenuous, indirect control over the local fishing population. Local bigwigs work for each of the two political parties in the village.[2] They are expected to produce votes at election time. In this way they are able to concentrate political favors in their own hands, and they are quick to take advantage of all new opportunities for self-aggrandizement.

The bigwigs maintain their position by pretending to have greatly outdistanced their peers in the village and by making themselves useful to the real sources of power in the county. A rudimentary knowledge of reading, writing, and simple arithmetic helps them to differentiate themselves from the lower class, from which they themselves have arisen, and which they constantly and publicly malign. More often than not, it is the local bigwigs who perpetuate the myth of the lazy, ignorant, and uncooperative peasant. Whereas the relationship between the peasant and the traditional elite is rather paternalistic, characterized by a high degree of dependency and trust, peasant ties with local bigwigs are built upon and maintained through fear. Although the lower classes live in the hope of change, the bigwigs view the maintenance of the status quo as vital to their own interests. This attitude has far-reaching implications for any discussion of technological innovation and change because the local bigwigs control the purse strings in Coqueiral, and it is they who have the innovating power. They use this power, however, solely for their own benefit, and they are careful to discourage any innovation which might eventually put a fellow townsman in a competitive position.[3]

One example of a local bigwig is the president of the Colônia de Pescadores, the area's chapter of the national fishermen's guild, who is also the village representative of the ruling political party in the county. Sr. Nilo was born in the village. His father was a fish hawker who also took on occasional wage work as a mason. Sr. Nilo learned to read, write, and do simple arithmetic during four years at the local public school. While still a young man, he changed his family name and moved into his own house, where he opened a small general store using money (under $100) he had obtained on loan from a *patrão*. With his earnings from the store, Sr. Nilo bought the first of a number of jangadas which he rents to fishermen on a one-half share basis. With another loan, he built two small cargo vessels for the shipment of sugar and salt to the state capital. Sr. Nilo also planted some coconut palms on land rented from the Church and, later, a grove of about five hundred palms on a narrow strip of land between the Guaiamu River and the sea, in front of the village of Baxias.[4]

In 1939, Sr. Nilo was made secretary of the newly established fishermen's guild, and in 1944 he assumed the presidency, when the former president moved to the state capital. In that same year, he married a young woman from the county seat and began selling lumber from her family's plantation. He borrowed more money from his mother-in-law to buy a truck. When his mother-in-law died, he managed to sell the truck for a considerable sum of money.[5] During this time, Sr. Nilo remained in the village, experimenting with a variety of fishing techniques, particularly with a *curral* (a large fish trap), a beach seine, and a hull sailboat. He eventually abandoned all of these experiments, blaming the failures on a lack of cooperation on the part of the fishermen. In 1963, on the advice of the owner of the sugar mill, Sr. Nilo, together with his brother-in-law, bought a small sugar plantation and a new truck. Again, this purchase was effected through a loan.

Although he enjoys a relatively high degree of mobility, the president of the fisherman's guild is a man who is not accepted by either the lower or upper class. He is despised by the fishermen for his constant harassment of them, and he is used but not accepted by the upper class. Although he has one of the better houses in the village and a standard of living considerably higher than the norm, Sr. Nilo is subject to the same social and recreational restrictions as the poorest of fishermen. He is not invited to the homes of the upper-class townsmen in Guaiamu, nor do the planters from the valley visit him in his home during their vacations in Coqueiral. At the same time, Sr. Nilo refuses to participate in the social life of the village. He does not watch the Sunday soccer matches or attend the performances of folk songs and dances which are popular with the fishermen. He is able to maintain his children in the county seat, but rather than have them walk the seven kilometers each way to the better school in Guaiamu, they are forced to live in an old, virtually unfurnished house, which formerly belonged to his in-laws. Sr. Nilo owns property, but he is in debt. He has a position, but at the expense of the fishermen. He derides them for laziness; yet, he himself is idle. The size of his operation requires that he spend only one day a week at his farm, except during the sugar harvest, and most of his time is spent loafing in the village.[6]

As president of the Colônia de Pescadores, Sr. Nilo reaps innumerable benefits from his position, the very least of which is his small percentage of the tax on fish. His earnings from the Colônia are actually quite small. As representative of the ruling political party in the county, however, he is able to obtain political favors in exchange for the promise of votes.[7] These favors are always distributed among his own kinsfolk, with whom he recently re-established ties. Thus, a nonfunctioning medical post built in 1951 was staffed quickly, with Sr. Nilo's three brothers acting as secretary, male nurse, and janitor. Each receives Cr$77,000 ($42) per month for his services, even though none of them has had any special training[8] and the post stopped functioning in 1960, when a doctor and dentist who had been living in Guaiamu moved away. The "male nurse" receives an additional Cr$7,000 ($3.80) per month for taking care of the diesel engine which, when not broken, provides electricity to approximately a fourth of the houses in Coqueiral. He also receives 30% of all land taxes, which he collects as agent for the Church. Furthermore, a nephew of Sr. Nilo receives Cr$4,000 ($2.20) for assisting with the diesel engine. Sr. Nilo's sister teaches in the grade school maintained by the fishermen's guild, and a niece teaches in the village public school. An uncle of his acts as tax collector for the fishermen's guild and for the mayor's office.

Such nepotism underlies the entire fabric of life in Coqueiral. At the lowest stratum of society, intrafamilial cooperation is essential for the survival of the community, and it is doubtful that anyone assuming the position of a local bigwig would behave differently. As we shall see, the leader of the political opposition certainly is no exception. Unfortunately, the power of the bigwigs, with its economic base, impinges heavily on the fishermen. None of the bigwigs in Coqueiral derives his principal livelihood from the productive end of fishing. Rather, they exploit the labors of fishermen and middlemen alike.

While the resources of the sea are open and free, strict controls are imposed on fishermen and middlemen on the shore. Fish hawkers are required to register with local officials in the county seat and to pay Cr$1,200 ($.60) per year for the privilege of selling fish in places designated by the mayor's office. Wholesale and retail prices of fish are set arbitrarily, and taxes are levied on both transactions. Fishermen pay a 10% tax in cash to the fishermen's guild on all fish weighed for sale above the first 3 kilos. Fish hawkers must pay Cr$2 (less than $.01) per kilo to the mayor's office. Species of fish are divided into four classes, which are accorded values based on consumers' tastes.[9] The difference in price, however, amounts to only Cr$100 ($.06) per kilo between each class of fish. Price controls are strictly maintained on first-class species in order to insure a supply of inexpensive, better-quality fish to the Guaiamu market. In this way, the local bigwigs hope to retain the favor of the planters from whom they derive their power. While second- and third-class species of fish are sold at comparable prices in other ports, first-class species of fish command twice the price elsewhere that they bring in Coqueiral. Obviously, there is no interest in supplying lesser-quality species of fish at lower prices to the local peasantry. Instead, price ceilings on first-class species of fish sharply limit the earnings of both fishermen and middlemen. As we shall see, the limitations imposed by the small consumer market preclude the effective use of middlemen.

Every fisherman eighteen years of age or older is required by Brazilian law to register with the local port captain and to receive from him a license to fish. At the same time, he must take out membership in the local chapter of the national fishermen's guild nearest to his port of embarkation. Many fishermen in Coqueiral both neglect to register with the port captain, who resides in Guaiamu, and fail to become members of the fishermen's guild, primarily because of the lack of benefits.

Registration with the local port captain theoretically makes a fisherman eligible for retirement pay from the Brazilian Maritime Institute. Pensions of Cr$26,000 ($15) per month are paid to men who have reached sixty-five years of age, completed thirty years of service, or are incapacitated. In order to be eligible for a pension a fisherman must make an annual payment of 8% of his minimum monthly salary, which is calculated on a yearly basis (Cr$39,600 [$22] in the state of Alagoas in 1965) from the time of matriculation in the Institute. Only twelve men in Coqueiral actually receive retirement benefits. Several other old men are eligible for pensions but are unable to pay their retroactive contributions, which date back to 1952, the year the law requiring registration was passed.

The Colônia de Pescadores Antônio Barnabé is the local chapter of the national fishermen's guild, established by federal law in 1938. The guild is administered on the state level by the Federação de Pescadores (Federation of Fishermen), and on the national level, by the Confederação Nacional de Pescadores (National Confederation of Fishermen). While the *colônias* were established as mutual aid societies, intended to provide assistance to the fishermen who voluntarily subscribed to them, they have failed in this task. Rather, the structure of the organization, based on the syndicalist ideology of Brazil's Estado Novo, lends itself to an archaic system of supervision and control.[10] By taking 10% in taxes on all earnings, refusing to extend credit, and dispensing a negligible amount of money for social assistance, the *colônias* clearly limit social mobility among the fishermen. Thus they serve only to maintain the rigid social structure that spawned them, and to systematically drain off earnings which might be used for innovation and change.

The administration of the local guild is through a board of three men who are supposed to be elected competitively every second year from among the membership. The current president, Sr. Nilo, has retained that office ever since 1944 by presenting himself and the other board members as a single slate for re-election. None of the officers pays membership dues to the Colônia, and not one is a fisherman. Despite the fact that federal law prohibits relatives from serving concurrently on the board, an uncle of Sr. Nilo serves as *fiscal*, or tax collector and treasurer. The secretary, responsible for keeping accounts, which must be submitted monthly to the state agency along with 3% of the Colônia's earnings, is employed at the sugar mill and returns to the village only occasionally to care for the books.

Membership in a fishermen's guild entails the monthly payment of dues and includes the stipulation that fishermen might mutually consent to pay up to 10% of their earnings to the guild, in anticipation of fringe benefits and credit. The dues in Coqueiral are Cr$50 ($.03) per month, and the full 10% tax on all fish weighed for sale above three kilos is imposed. Forty per cent of the earnings of the Colônia, or 4% of all fish weighed for sale above three kilos, is taken in salaries by the officials of the guild. The president receives 10%, the secretary, 5%, and the *fiscal*, a flat 25%. In addition, the *fiscal* earns 25% of the Cr$2 per kilo tax levied on fish hawkers by the mayor's office.

Both fishermen and fish hawkers bitterly resent the imposition of taxes and price ceilings. They know that fishermen in other parts of the nation, particularly in urban areas, receive a far higher price for their fish. They argue that the regular meetings required by law for a public accounting of funds are not held, and that the officials receive a salary at the expense of the fishermen although they perform no service other than tax collecting. They argue further that neither the owners of the large beach seines nor the fishermen on other beaches included in the zone supervised by the Colônia de Pescadores in Coqueiral are obliged to pay taxes. The former are local coconut growers, and the latter have long since left the Colônia, to which they paid taxes without receiving compensatory benefits. The officials of the Colônia are unable to enforce their regulations fully because it is difficult to travel to the other beaches.

In like vein, the fishermen of Coqueiral are loath to pay taxes for benefits that are rarely forthcoming. This is reflected by a sharply decreasing membership in the Colônia. Although 153 persons were on the roll in 1965, only 45 of the 85 active fishermen in Coqueiral were members. The other 108 members listed lived in other villages in the area. A total of 53 members attended the election meeting during that year. Of even greater significance is the fact that only 28 members of the Colônia paid any dues at all in 1965. Moreover, in October, 1965,

48 fishermen owed taxes on about 1,770 kilos of fish, some of this nearly two years overdue. The value of these taxes was estimated at more than Cr$500,000 ($280), and the president made every effort to collect the money. In addition, fish hawkers owed taxes to the county on over 5,000 kilos of fish, but the *fiscal* insisted in vain on payment.

In 1964 fringe benefits to fishermen amounted to only Cr$18,900 ($10); no money was loaned for the purchase of equipment. Yet, in the same year the Colônia received over Cr$104,429 ($57) in taxes and dues alone. In the seven-month period from January to June, 1965, the Colônia netted Cr$128,680 ($71) in taxes and dues. An additional Cr$200,000 ($110) was received from state deputies for the construction of a building to house the weigh-in scale. Cr$30,000 ($16) more was received from the state for the Colônia's school. During that period, a mere Cr$7,000 ($3.80) was given to fishermen in fringe benefits, while Cr$400,000 ($220) was spent on the construction of a market which fishermen were forbidden to enter. The Colônia sponsored a St. Peter's Day dance that cost Cr$20,260 ($11), most of which was spent for the band and the electricity. A statement issued by the president of the Colônia in July, 1965, claimed debts in the amount of Cr$100,000 ($55), which he said had been borrowed at interest from his brother, the "male nurse," and he urged the fishermen to pay their delinquent taxes and dues. Table 5 lists the income and expenditures of the Colônia in 1965.

TABLE 5. INCOME AND EXPENDITURES OF THE
COLONIA DE PESCADORES ANTONIO BARNABÉ

INCOME		EXPENSES	
Taxes	Cr$114,300	State Agency	Cr$3,300
Dues	14,380	Fringe Benefits	7,000
Gifts	200,000	Construction	400,000
Federal Aid	30,000	Dance	20,260
		Salaries	44,400
		School Maintenance	21,870
Total	Cr$358,680		Cr$496,830
	($200)		($276)

The president of the Colônia complains about the lack of cooperation on the part of fishermen and periodically threatens to take away fishing privileges for nonpayment of dues and taxes. Instances of police reprisals add credence to his orders. Fishermen cite innumerable cases in which police were called to town from Guaiamu to haul away a reluctant fisherman. For their part, the fishermen complain about the loss of benefits over the years, and they blame such losses on the present administration. Still, the records indicate that the Colônia has been only slightly more generous in years gone by. In 1955, 15% of the intake from taxes and dues was returned to the fishermen in the form of fringe benefits, as opposed to 18% in 1964. The total given out to fishermen in the first seven months of 1965 was slightly over 5% (see Table 6).

TABLE 6. INCOME AND FRINGE BENEFITS OF THE
COLONIA DE PESCADORES ANTONIO BARNABÉ

FISCAL YEAR	INCOME FROM TAXES AND DUES	FRINGE BENEFITS	PERCENTAGE
1955	Cr$29,691	Cr$4,660	15%
1964	104,429	18,900	18%
1965 (April-Nov.)	128,680	7,000	5%

Growing disaffection with the Colônia is apparent in the fact that a mere twenty fishermen showed up on St. Peter's Day for the blessing of the fish market built to house the weigh-in scale. The others complained bitterly that the building was erected "only for the fish to stain." At the dance that night, Sr. Nilo sided with intruders from the county seat, who proceeded to break up the dance. Elderly fishermen claim that earnings from fishing were higher before the Colônia brought the scale to the beach and began to tax fish. Previously, it was customary to give one fish in ten to the Church,[11] and the alleged diminishing returns in fishing are held to be a "punishment from God" for neglecting this old custom.

A credit and loan association was formed in 1964 in Coqueiral. The founders were mostly retired fishermen who were completely disaffected from the Colônia de Pescadores. Because of the need to staff the board of directors with officers who could read, write, and keep the accounts, the executive of the Associação Beneficente de Coqueiral (Benevolent Society) was entrusted to the party leader of the local political opposition in the village. Like the president of the Colônia de Pescadores, Sr. Mario is also a local bigwig who does not have the interest of the fishermen at heart.

Sr. Mario was born to lower-class parents in the village, but was reared by a childless coconut planter from whom he later inherited extensive groves. He is the largest single coconut planter in Coqueiral, and he rents the most sizable landholdings from the Church. He supplements his income with a large beach seine and several rafts, which he rents to fishermen for a half share of the catch. When seeking pre-election support in the village for his party's candidate, Sr. Mario promised that if elected, his candidate would provide financial aid to the newly-formed Benevolent Society, a promise which went unfulfilled during the first year of the Society's existence. In an attempt to build his own political base, Sr. Mario accepted the job as secretary of the Society. He appointed his son, a student in the state capital, as treasurer. A friend, who makes his living both as a planter with a thousand coconut trees and as the owner of a small farm, was elected president. Sr. Mario and his friend are also partners in a nylon gill net which they rent on a share system.

The new board of directors, acting out of self-interest, quickly transformed the Society into a loan agency. Within one year of its existence they parleyed the Cr$500 ($.28) monthly dues of the fifteen members into a capital fund of Cr$100,000 ($55). Yet, no fringe benefits were granted to the membership, and interest rates on loans were charged at the rate of 5% per month for members and 10% per month for non-members. Although the founders of the Society had specifically agreed that no member of the board of directors would receive a salary—this being one of the chief points of contention in the case of the Colônia de Pescadores—Sr. Mario soon declared that 20% of all interest paid to the Society would be fair recompense for the work of his son, the absentee treasurer. The secretary and the president did not receive any salary themselves. It soon came to light, however, that Sr. Mario was the Society's principal borrower. By seeing to it that his own interest payments never exceeded the income his son derived from the interest on others' loans, Sr. Mario was supplied with a ready source of liquid capital which ultimately could pay for the boy's expenses in the city.

As in the case of the Colônia de Pescadores, it is the fishermen who suffer from the maneuverings of these local bigwigs. In both cases, capital is either drained off in taxes or utilized for nonfishing endeavors. Neither the Colônia nor the Society makes money available to fishermen for investment in new techniques. Then too, the replacement of old equipment is becoming increasingly difficult. There is no agency outside the village that is willing to risk capital against the sporadic earnings of fishermen. Only the local bigwigs, utilizing capital from other interests, are in a position to invest in a variety of fishing equipment, providing, of course, that they can count on the labor of their impoverished fellow villagers. Yet, until now the fishermen have been able to maintain themselves as independent producers, and the commercialization and exploitation of both human and natural resources has been minimized.

Stratification and Productive Technology

THERE ARE four major types of fishing practiced in Coqueiral. The first, and the most important in terms of the number of independent participants, is hook-and-line fishing from log rafts at sea. The second, and the most important in terms of potential yield, is fishing with large beach seines, which are set out from rafts and pulled to shore. A third type of fishing, which is becoming more popular, involves the use of nylon gill nets from log rafts within the bay. Finally, a variety of subsistence fishing techniques are used in the shallow waters off the beach, and these are not without their commercial aspects.

Preferences among the types of fishing are governed by a number of factors. First, there are factors of an economic order, namely, comparative yields vs. comparative costs. However, not all techniques are available to all fishermen. While almost everyone can afford hooks and line and a small raft for fishing, only men with outside capitalization can purchase and maintain large nets. Secondly, there are ecological factors. Changes in wind, weather, and the seasonal run of various kinds of fish affect both the choice of fishing techniques and the constitution of crews at different times of year. Ecological factors act upon the market and affect economic decisions. The market is also conditioned by a variety of demographic and social structural factors and by the seasonal appearance of different species of fish. It is the type of equipment, however—and not the type of craft—which is the most important variable in successful fishing for the independent producer.

The stock of equipment available to a fisherman determines the extent to which he can successfully exploit the resources of the sea. By utilizing several types of nets in addition to hooks and line, the fishermen of Coqueiral are able to exploit a wide variety of species, which inhabit the area at different times of year. Still, not all types of equipment are immediately available to all fishermen, and some have a far better earning potential than others. To sit patiently with hook and line in a great expanse of ocean is not nearly as effective a technique for catching fish as encircling a large shoal with a net. Differential access to various fishing techniques depends largely on one's ability to accumulate capital or to arrange for credit; and the ownership of equipment in Coqueiral depends on sources of wealth derived from nonfishing activities.

Even the large group of independent producers who fish by hook and line on their own relatively inexpensive log rafts depends on other household income for the replacement of their craft. While primitive technology, limited production, and strict controls on fish prices preclude the possibility of peasant fishermen earning large sums of money, small log rafts are always within the reach of most fishermen. By combining the incomes of several members of fishing households, a large number of independent producers are able to fish on their own jangadas during at least part of the year. Before discussing the combination of economic and ecological factors that make possible a choice between fishing in a crew or independently, it is first necessary to point out the differential access to other kinds of equipment available in the village.

There are some types of fishing equipment that are relatively expensive and thus are not available to peasant fishermen. The use of beach seines, for example, requires a sizable amount of capital in local terms, and the services of both a fixed crew on a raft and a large number of people on the shore. Such seines are owned and operated by entrepreneurs, who derive their regular income from nonfishing activities and use the nets as a means to supplement their incomes during the summer fishing season.[1] They exploit a large labor force of impoverished people who have to resort to subsistence fishing with equipment that is not their own.

BEACH SEINE

The *rêde de arrasto* (beach seine) is a variety of large pocket seine. It is approximately six hundred meters long and fourteen meters high at its center, diminishing in height to some nine meters at each end. A sacklike pocket is formed in the center of the net as it is hauled to shore. There are three beach seines of this size in Coqueiral and one that is slightly smaller, measuring some five hundred meters in length. The mesh at the center, made from a cotton fiber, measures some two to three centimeters, becoming larger in the sleeves, which are made from a vegetable fiber called *ticum (Bactris setosa mart.)*.

As stated above, the original cost and upkeep of the beach seines place them out of the reach of most fishermen in Coqueiral. All of the owners of seines are farmers or coconut planters, who draw the cost of the net and its upkeep from capital obtained from nonfishing interests. The three large nets are owned respectively by two brothers and their brother-in-law, who is Sr. Mario, secretary of the Benevolent Society. One of the two brothers, Sr. João, inherited his net from his father. The other, Sr. Antônio, bought his seine with earnings from the largest dry goods store in the village, plus fifty *tarefas* of land, and over seven hundred coconut trees. The small beach seine is owned by an agriculturalist who rents seven *tarefas* of land and owns more than one hundred fifty coconut trees.

The larger nets each took two people about six months to make and cost over Cr$1,250,000 ($640). In addition, a large jangada, costing approximately Cr$180,000 ($100) is required to set the net, while a drying rack and storage hut, estimated at approximately Cr$90,000 ($50) are necessary for its maintenance. The total cost of a large beach seine then, is Cr$1,520,000 ($820).

Major repairs are, for the most part, done by hired day labor, and the cost of upkeep is very high. There is the constant danger that a net will tear on a rock or that fish caught inside will rip through the mesh. Repairs for Sr. João's beach seine in the 1964–65 fishing season came to more than one-fifth the cost of a new net. Sr. João, who has a limited income from some four hundred coconut trees, insisted that he would retire his net after the following fishing season unless a compensatory catch was yielded.

Although beach seines are used for commercial speculation, there is no guarantee that earnings will be high. Fishing is done primarily in the summer, when shoals of mackerel enter the bay from the north. While catches up to 15,000 fish in a single casting were reported for one summer, the season lasts only four or five months (November to Feb-

Shore crew hauling in a pocket seine

ruary). Moreover, net fishing is not done every day, even in the height of the summer season, and several days at a time can be lost while a net is being repaired. Very large catches are said to have been given away to prevent an easily saturated market. In the seven months of my ethnographic research in the village (April to November), the nets were used on only nine occasions. The largest daily catch recorded for a single net during this time amounted to 520 first class fish, weighing from 1 to 2 kilos apiece. This involved three castings, or *lanços*, one of which captured only twenty fish. A *lanço* requires approximately one and one-half hours to complete. Time is also spent waiting in between *lanços* for the next shoal to appear or for another net crew to complete its "pull" to the shore.

All shoals entering the bay are shared between the four nets in operation. This sharing is accomplished by spacing the four rafts about two hundred yards apart, starting at the end of the inshore reef, which marks the entrance to the bay. The first raft out has the choice of positions, the spot closest to the reef being preferred. The reef position does not guarantee the largest catch, however, since the main body of the shoal may not be the first into the bay. Each group has access to the shoal that passes on its right. As each raft begins to encircle a shoal, dropping its net in the water while still under oar, the next raft moves over to occupy the vacated position, awaiting its own turn. On one occasion, three rafts made several *lanços* each, while the fourth never left the position it had taken up at the end of the reef.

Each raft is manned by an eight-man crew *(os homens do maré)* comprised of a captain, four rowers, two net men, and a rope man. While crews supposedly have a fixed membership, the personnel were never the same on more than two consecutive days during the 1965 winter season. It must be noted, however, that net fishing very rarely is undertaken in winter, when rough seas are common. Occasionally a shoal of fish is sighted and crews are assembled haphazardly on the beach by blowing on a conch horn. In the summer months, when cool dry nights and an onshore breeze signify the clearing of the waters in the bay, preparations for the next day's fishing are made during the night, and the crew, while not fixed, is at least more regular.

At least thirty *homens da terra* (shore crew) are required to haul the huge net to shore. Up to sixty people have been observed pulling in a

beach seine at one time. While custom prohibits the constant switch-
ing from one net to another, even on different days, there is no longer
any rigid system of identification, such as the *fichas*, or tickets, which
were previously required by the owners for one to gain access to a net.

The catch is divided on a share system, as indicated in Table 7. The
captain begins by setting aside approximately 10% of the catch for the
raft crew. In the one case in which the captain is not the owner of the
net, he has first choice of the eight piles made from this selection. The
remaining fish are then laid out in two piles, one for the owner of the
net and the other for distribution among all other participants. Each
share, or *quinhão*, is based on the estimated size of fish rather than on
the actual weight. Ideally each of those who participate in hauling in
the net receives a share. On days when the nets were put out, everyone
showed special concern that the catch be divided equally. Two or more
children were told to share one *quinhão* between them. The owner
frequently offers his share to someone who helps him with the repair
of the net. In the one instance in which the owner of a net fishes as
part of the crew but is not the captain, he contributes his fisherman's
share to his captain.

TABLE 7. SAMPLE DISTRIBUTION OF BEACH SEINE CATCH

PERSONNEL	NUMBER OF SHARES	NUMBER OF FISH	PERCENTAGE OF CATCH
Owner	1	234	45%
Raft crew	8	52	10%
Total crew (Raft and shore)	68	234	45%

While the meager earnings of the shore crew on these nets often do
not suffice even for a single day's nutrition, villagers constantly return
to the nets for lack of other opportunities. Trying one's luck at net
fishing is considered far better than spending a day in the mangrove
swamp in search of crabs or mollusks. Even on days when the net
brings in so little that there is not enough for everyone who fishes to
receive a share, the shore crew still returns in the hope that the next
lanço will bring in a sizable catch.

LAMBUDA

The *lambuda* is a small pocket seine some two hundred meters in length, ten meters high at its center, and approximately five meters high at the ends. The mesh is considerably smaller than that of the larger beach seines, and these nets theoretically have been outlawed along the coast because they trap varieties of tiny fish, mostly of unprofitable third-class species. There are four such nets owned in Coqueiral, and several others from nearby communities are sometimes seen fishing at the other end of the beach, near the mouth of the Guaiamu River. Each *lambuda* costs approximately Cr$500,000 ($277) to make. A net house and a smaller drying rack, as well as a jangada, costing altogether some Cr$150,000 ($83) are required to set and maintain the net. While repairs on the larger nets are usually hired out, the owners of *lambudas* do their own mending. Still, the cost of materials is high.

Although it is considerably cheaper than the large *rêde de arrasto*, the *lambuda* is also beyond the reach of most of Coqueiral's fishermen. All of the owners make their living from something other than fishing. One *lambuda* is owned by Sr. João, who also has a large beach seine. A storekeeper owns another. Two *lambuda* owners are retired fishermen on monthly pensions, one of whom supplements his income with earnings from building jangadas.

The *lambuda* is set out all year long, and one can be seen on the beach nearly every day. The setting and pulling of the net takes about an hour, and as many as six *lanços* were counted in a day. Still, the catches are small and rarely of commercial value. Six people make up the regular raft crew, including a captain, two oarsmen, two netmen, and a man on the rope. This net is easily pulled in by eight people onshore. Women and young men make up the shore crews of most *lambudas*. The catch is divided up in the same manner as that of the *rêde de arrasto*, with the exception that even the tiny fish caught are divided among the participants. In the case of the larger beach seine, tiny fish brought in with the seaweed that comes with each haul are left for small children to collect on the beach. The crew of a *lambuda* rarely have fish left to sell, although on occasion the owner of the net sells a few of the larger fish from the catch. All shrimp caught in the *lambuda* belong exclusively to the owner for sale as bait.

CACEIA

The *caceia*, or gill net, is a rectangular net approximately one hundred meters long and three meters high, which is set adrift from a raft and left upright in the water at a point marked by a buoy. *Caceias* made from *ticum* have long been known in Coqueiral, but the gill nets made from nylon that began to enter the village in the summer of 1965 are much preferred. The nylon net is a great improvement over the *ticum* net, in terms of both strength and durability and the size of the catch, since it proves invisible to fish, which get entangled in it. Although gill nets catch mostly *caçao bico doce (Mustelis canis)* or smooth dogfish sharks, of second- and third-class market varieties,[2] they seem far more expedient than handlines. The traditional elites and local bigwigs do not like to eat dogfish, but the fishermen claim a taste for it. The catch from *caceias* is sold easily, and the nets are becoming extremely popular. Even the "male nurse" bought one in the hope of catching mackerel and other better-quality species of fish, which travel mid-water in shoals during the summer season. Within a year, seven nets came into use in Coqueiral, and the introduction of at least fourteen more is anticipated.

Although the first two nets were purchased by local landowners and subsequent nets were financed with capital from outside the village, the *caceia* is potentially within the reach of every fisherman in Coqueiral, especially if some initial financing could be found. A ready-made gill net costs only about Cr$100,000 ($55), although one can be made by hand for considerably less cash output. Repairs are done by the owners, themselves, and neither drying racks nor a hut for storage are necessary. A small raft which can be rowed to the outer reefs is necessary for casting.

It is interesting to note that one of the owners of a *caceia* is a recent arrival from the town of Jitaí, on the Jitaí Lagoon to the north, who came to Coqueiral to live with his daughter and son-in-law, the "male nurse." He brought with him a new dugout canoe, which he used for fishing in the lagoon. The canoe proved totally unadaptable to the conditions in the bay at Coqueiral, however, and was constantly tipping over. In a vain attempt to stabilize it, he added buoyant logs to either side of the dugout. Discouraged by his failure, he planned to abandon the canoe and continue to set his gill net from a raft that he would build for the purpose.

The gill nets are capable of fishing all year round, irrespective of seasonal changes. Therefore considerable increases in over-all production can be anticipated. During a one-month period in July and August, a jangada fishing with two *caceias* yielded some 287 kilos. The average per day catch was 11.5 kilos—well above that for handlining in the same period. The gill nets also were used to fish twenty-five days in a thirty-day period, as compared with eighteen days for a handlining crew on a regular jangada. The gill nets are owned by two sets of partners, one by a group of fourteen small landowners from Guaiamu, and the other, jointly by the secretary and the president of the Benevolent Society. The former group were less intent on market sales than on their own dietary needs, and the tremendous amount of food reserved from each catch for home consumption by the fourteen partners and two crew members greatly detracted from their possible earnings.

TABLE 8. PRODUCTION STATISTICS FOR RAFT FISHING WITH
TWO GILL NETS
(July 10 to August 10, 1965)

Number of days at sea 25
Number of days with recorded catch 25
Number of hours under sail 90
Number of hours fishing 148
Number of days seeking first-class fish 5
    Average hours under sail 4.6
    Average hours fishing 6
    Total kilos caught 27
    Kilos sold 7
      Earnings ....Cr$2,800 ($1.50)
Number of days seeking second-class fish........... 20
    Average hours under sail 3
    Average hours fishing 6
    Total kilos caught 260
    Kilos sold 160
      Earnings ....Cr$48,000 ($26)
Total Earnings ....Cr$50,800 ($27.50)

So significant were the earnings of a gill net fisherman on another raft, however, that in three summer months he was able to pay off a Cr$15,000 ($83) loan for the purchase of the *caceia*, and then to borrow an equal amount in order to buy a second *caceia*. Both loans came from a wealthy summer resident who acts as his *patrão*. At the end of five months, he moved from his wattle-and-daub shack with its thatched roof into a lime-fronted and tile-roofed dwelling on the main street of town. At the same time, he joined less and less in the conversational groups of fishermen in the huts along the beach and appeared more frequently under the tamarind tree at the end of the main street, which is the favorite gathering place of the local bigwigs.

To return to the economics of the catch, gill net fishing requires a crew of two men, including a captain, and a fisherman who helps to set and retrieve the net. Division of the catch is based on a half-share, or *meiação*, system, by which the owner and the crew receive equal shares if the owner himself does not fish. When the owner does fish, the division of the catch is in three parts: one for the net, one for the boat, and a third which is divided among the crew. The owner's expenses for feeding the crew are always taken out before the catch is divided.

Fishing with gill nets offers a potentially large increase in over-all production in the village, as well as sizable increments in the earnings of individual fishermen. Still, resistance to the new technique is being vocalized by Sr. Nilo, president of the Colônia de Pescadores, who complains about the low quality of fish that the gill nets bring in, despite the fact that his own brother owns one. He would prefer that fishermen continue to use hooks and line to catch better qualities of fish, which cost only $.06 more per kilo to buy. He attempts to play down the effectiveness of the gill net and to discourage its use by telling fishermen that it is not a money-maker. More important, the Colônia extends no loans to fishermen for the purchase of gill nets.

OTHER FISHING TECHNIQUES

In addition to net fishing and handlining, a variety of secondary fishing techniques are of importance in the economy of Coqueiral and indicate the fishermen's desire to exploit marine resources as fully as possible.

Turtle fishing has the highest commercial value and therefore is the most significant among these techniques.

The turtle hunt takes place on the outer reefs, where the turtles surface during low tide. A small, oar-propelled raft *(bote)* is towed out to sea by a sail-driven jangada. Besides the captain of the large jangada, the hunting crew consists of a harpoonist, considered to be a specialist, and an oarsman, who rows the *bote* along the edge of the reef. The turtle is harpooned with a thrust through his shell and, after a lengthy chase, is brought aboard the larger raft and transported live to the shore. In the course of the hunt the waiting jangada does not fish, but stands ready to pursue the *bote,* if need be. The captain of the larger raft hopes that the turtle catch will compensate for the day's absence from the fishing grounds. As many as three turtles, weighing several hundred kilos, are brought ashore from a single hunt. The catch is divided in thirds: one for the raft, one for the harpoonist, and one to be shared among the crew. The raft used may belong to any one of a number of the regular fishermen in the village. The two turtle hunters own no equipment other than the harpoon, and when they are not hired out for a hunt they work as coconut harvesters. For the raft fishermen, turtle fishing serves as a supplement to their regular income and as an occasional variation in their work routine.

Turtle fins are used as bait for shark fishing in the deep waters along the outer reefs. A large iron hook is attached to iron chain links, which in turn are attached midway on a long rope anchored to the ocean floor and marked with a buoy. A light tug on the buoy tells an inspecting crew if a shark has taken the hook. The shark meat is sold, as is the oil made from the liver. Only one man in the village goes shark fishing regularly. Anyone may go along as his crew. The catch is split in two equal parts *(meiação)*, but all of the oil is kept by the man who owns the hook. The owner is required to discount approximately 10% of the weight sold to fish hawkers because of the weight loss that results from the removal of the shark's hide. While sizable catches have been reported, only one shark, measuring some two meters in length, was brought ashore during the period of my research in the village.

On nights when the tide is low and the moon is new, the outer reefs also are the scene of lobster fishing. This is the favorite sporting pastime of sugar planters when they visit the village. Several jangadas sail out, and fishermen, lighting up the reef with torches made from straw, collect the small, spiny lobsters that run along the reef. Occasionally, fishermen from Coqueiral sail out after lobsters, which they sell in the village. While it has some commercial value, lobster fishing is considered more of a sport, and the excursion usually is climaxed by *cachaça* and a cookout.

SUBSISTENCE FISHING

Other fishing activities are carried on solely as a means of supplementing the villagers' diet. Although the villagers have ready access to the mangrove swamp where soft shell crabs abound, no one exploits them commercially, as is done now on a very large scale in the neighboring village of Estrada Velha. The mangrove swamp provides a wealth of high-protein foods for domestic consumption; and in the winter months particularly, women and children go there almost every day in search of oysters, mussels, clams, and crabs. Once in a while these shellfish are sold from door to door in the village.

Additional dietary supplements are obtained through reef fishing and gathering. Several young men go reef fishing almost daily with four-foot poles fitted out with six feet of line tied at the end to a single hook. They catch third- and fourth-class species of fish, which are of little commercial value. Some men go surf casting with bamboo poles and weighted lines along the eastern shore beyond the end of the reef. An occasional moray eel or small octopus is picked up near the reef. These activities increase in the winter months and on days when bad weather does not permit the rafts to sail. Young girls and, now and then, a woman, will gather small crabs, or *aratú (Coniopsis cruentatus)*, which inhabit the reef. At times, young men and women make a reef excursion together to collect sea urchins, which they roast and eat on the spot.

SUBSISTENCE AND ENTREPRENEURSHIP

At this point it is essential to note that even among subsistence producers in a fishing economy there appears to be a reservoir of entre-

preneurial talent. Many fishermen have learned to exploit the catching
of bait, since the fishermen of Coqueiral are always willing to pay for
bait, either in cash or with a percentage of their catch. A steady supply
of bait is also a major incentive in attracting fishermen to certain middlemen during the summer months, when bait is especially scarce.

In the winter months, shrimp is used to catch *ubarana* (*Elops
saurus*), or ladyfish, which is encountered on the way to the fishing
grounds, where it is then cut and used as bait. During this time of year,
various shrimping techniques are employed, usually by the fishermen
themselves. A single fisherman, using a *jereré*, or dip net, can catch
shrimp or tiny fish by pushing the net along the muddy floor of the
river or mangrove swamp. A *teteá*, or *tikúka*, is a smaller dip net used
for the same purpose. A *redinha*, or rectangular drag net, also is dragged
along a mud bottom for shrimp, but requires two men working to-
gather to drag it in. Sometimes a crew goes out together for *isca*; sometimes a fisherman and his son can be seen heading down the beach during low tide with a net and a straw torch for fending off mosquitos.
Reluctance on the part of a fisherman to help catch bait is frequently
the cause of quarrels. If a fisherman has no one to help him catch bait,
he is forced to buy it for cash from a *lambuda* owner.

In the summer months, when the *ubarana* moves away from the
coast and out of the range of Coqueiral's fishermen, *tainha* (*Mugil
brasiliensis*), or mullet, is used as bait for the *cavala* (*Scomber colias*),
or Spanish mackerel, which, in turn, is used to catch first-class fish. The
fact that *cavala* is used for bait, regardless of its own high commercial
value, gives further indication of the market limits on first-class species
and also of the inadequate techniques for preservation of the catch.
In the summer calm and when winds prevail from the northeast,
cavala is caught on trawl lines as the rafts sail out to the fishing grounds.

Tainha is trapped in a *tarrafa*, or cast net, which is a conico-circular
net approximately 170 inches in length, with a 480-inch circular bottom weighted down with small lead weights. The net is cast in shallow
waters by a professional *tarrafeiro* whose wide, sweeping motion causes
it to open in the air before hitting the water and sinking to the bottom.
The *tarrafa* is then drawn slowly out of the water in a gradual lifting
motion that closes the net on the fish trapped within it.

The *tarrafa* is used widely in the village by fishermen who cast merely

Baiting for shrimp with a dip net

for food to eat in the winter months and by those who fish for bait to sell in the summer. There are three *isqueiros,* or bait suppliers, in Coqueiral who spend the winter months at occasional day labor or collecting and husking coconuts. At low tide they can be seen either in the shallow pools within the inshore reef or along the beach, casting their *tarrafas* for a small herring or anchovy for the day's meal. During the summer, they become entrepreneurs who supply their catch as bait, in anticipation of a percentage of any fish caught. The *tarrafeiro* turned *isqueiro* receives 10% of the catch, paid in cash by the owner of the raft, and a choice of fish to eat.

While *tarrafa* fishing in itself represents a subsistence activity with little cash value attached to the catch, baiting is an entrepreneurial activity involving a high risk, which necessitates the maintenance of a number of subsidiary occupations on the part of the *isqueiro.* In several cases, *isqueiros* use their bait catching to attract raft fishermen who will supply them, in turn, with salable fish, particularly in the summer months.

[V]

The Nature of Raft Fishing

THE MAJORITY of fishermen in Coqueiral earn their livelihood by alternating between fishing independently from their own log rafts and serving as crew members on jangadas belonging to someone else. This alternation is influenced by both economic and ecological factors. The appearance of particular species of fish, correlated with the current supply on the market, dictates, for the most part, the techniques in use and the choice of one type of raft over another within given seasons. On the one hand, the demands and limitations of the market play an important role in the seasonal selection of fishing equipment. On the other hand, limited earnings necessarily reinforce the selection of certain types of equipment.

Jangada fishermen are able to exploit the entire range of coastal fishing because variations in the basic design of the rafts permit jangadeiros to sail over a relatively large area of ocean above the continental shelf in all seasons. The rafts vary according to size, method of propulsion, and accoutrements; and the resultant types are utilized on different fishing grounds and in different seasons.

Two basic fishing patterns can be distinguished. First, large jangadas sail beyond the outer reef, often to the edge of the continental shelf, where they fish in waters up to two hundred fathoms deep for the larger and scarcer rock-living species that have first-class market values. Second, smaller rafts, called *botes*, fish within the ten-mile limit of the outer reef in waters up to fifty meters in depth for smaller, but far more abundant second-class species of fish. A medium-sized raft, called a *paquete*, alternates between the two fishing patterns as weather conditions permit.

The *jangada de alto* (raft of the high seas) is used primarily in fishing for rock-living species at the edge of the continental shelf, mainly

61

during the Lenten period and in the summer months when tourist demands for first-class fish are high. Although the *jangada de alto* is propelled by a large lateen sail, its sailing time is long, often up to six hours or more to reach the most distant fishing spots. For this reason, a salting platform and other means for preserving the catch are required. The distance of the fishing grounds from shore sometimes makes it necessary for the crew to spend more than one day at sea, sleeping on the *salgadeira* and on the captain's bench, which explains the alternate name for this type of raft, the *jangada de dormida*.

The *paquete* has the same parts as a *jangada de alto* but differs from the latter in size. It is made from six logs, each approximately six meters long and slightly over one meter wide. While it is not as heavy, as stable, or as speedy, a *paquete* is capable of fishing the same general area as a *jangada de alto*. A *paquete* is less likely to sail out to the edge of the continental shelf in rough weather, although occasionally one does stay out overnight when weather permits. In the winter months, a *paquete* fishes for second-class species of fish closer into shore.

A small raft between three and four meters long and about one meter wide, made of four logs, and called a *bote de remo*, completes the stock of jangadas. It is equipped with only a basket, a forked staff, an anchor, and a bench on which a lone fisherman sits and rows. Some of the rafts of this type, called *botes à vela* (sailing rafts), are equipped with small lateen sails, which afford greater maneuverability and ease of operation. Both types of *botes* are used in all seasons, except on those winter days when the prevailing winds and strength of the currents prohibit a single fisherman from rowing out to sea. They are used most often in the summer, when second-class species of fish migrate southward and appear in large numbers just behind the inshore reef.

The choice of fishing pattern is affected not only by the seasonal migration of species of fish, but also by daily changes in climatic conditions. While the effect of the tides is minimal on rafts, which can be rolled to the water's edge with ease, the weather does influence the fishing pattern. Broadly speaking, there are three distinct fishing seasons—winter, summer, and the Lenten period (Figure 2).

The winter season generally lasts from May to August and is considered the worst time for fishing. Strong south or southeast winds are

FIGURE 2. SEASONAL FISHING PATTERNS

	SUMMER Jan.-Feb.	LENT March-April	WINTER May-June-July-August	SUMMER Sept.-Oct.-Nov.-Dec.
WIND	Gentle sea and shore breezes (westerly).		Strong winds from the south.	Steady northeasterly breeze.
CURRENTS	"Still" waters, soft currents.		Strong currents from the south.*	Steady currents from the north. ("Volta das aguas," or return of the waters.)
FISHING GROUNDS		Best months to fish the grounds at the edge of the continental shelf, in the general area of Coqueiral.	Northern fishing grounds for first-class species. Second-class banks within the outer reef.	Southern fishing grounds for first-class species. Harvest of second-class species behind inshore reef.
FISH		Spanish mackerel, yellowtail, sea bass (other first-class species).	Catfish (from the pluvial waters to the south), smooth dog, etc.	Barbudo, hake, mackerel (other first-class species).
EQUIPMENT		Beach seines, lambudas, jangada de alto, paquete.	Paquete, bote, lambudas.	Beach seines, lambudas, bote, jangada de alto, paquete.

TIME

	LENT Leave	LENT Return	WINTER Leave	WINTER Return	SUMMER Leave	SUMMER Return
Jangada	3 A.M.	5 P.M.	11 A.M.	11 P.M.	3 A.M.	4 P.M.
	7 A.M.	4 P.M. (next day)				
Paquete	4 A.M.	11 A.M.	11 A.M.	11 P.M.	5 A.M.	noon
Bote	6 A.M.	noon	8 A.M.	3 P.M.	4 A.M.	10 A.M.

* Two bottles found on shore. 1) Released ca. 220 kms. south of Capetown, South Africa, on May 13, 1964. Arrived Coqueiral on April 27, 1965. 2) Released on June 28, 1965 at 19°n.–30°w. (Dakar) and arrived Coqueiral on July 15, 1965.

accompanied by fast currents which bring to the bay the silted waters of the São Francisco River. During this season, the choice of fishing grounds is prescribed by daily weather conditions. It is extremely rare for rafts to stay out overnight in the winter season, and most fishing, even on *jangadas de alto*, is done for second-class species of fish. Both larger jangadas and *paquetes* fish for *bagre* (*Tachysurus sp.*) or catfish, in the silted waters just within the inner reef. Conditions often prohibit the use of small, oar-driven rafts. When they go out at all the *botes* stay well within the inner reef and catch only little fish for home consumption. Most of the owners of *botes* seek a place instead on the bow of a larger raft. When weather permits, a few fishermen take advantage of the prevailing winds to fish for first-class species on the rocky-bottom grounds north of the village.

The summer season begins in early September when the winds begin to shift to the northeast and currents start to run south again, clearing the waters around Coqueiral of the silt from the river. The *volta das aguas* (return of the waters) is accompanied by the migration of a second-class species of fish, *barbudo (Polynemus virginicus)*,[1] to the eastern shoreline just behind the inshore reef. In summer, large jangadas go out to the edge of the continental shelf more often to fish for first-class species. *Paquetes* and *botes* take advantage of the early morning land breezes to sail offshore, returning by midday with their baskets brimming with *barbudo*. In the early afternoon the sea breeze abates, and those fishermen who are still out near the reefs have to leave their small sailing rafts and *botes de remo* on the northern beaches between Coqueiral and Lagôa Sêca and walk back to the village.

In January, the northeast winds cease to blow, and the waters off Coqueiral are clear and calm. It is at this time that the shoals of mackerel begin to enter the bay and the large beach seines become a common sight. *Paquetes*, too small to stay out overnight, sail to the edge of the continental shelf and return the same day.[2] Despite the activity of the beach seines and the traffic to the outer fishing grounds, the majority of fish caught during the summer months are, like the winter catch, of second-class variety. Undoubtedly this is because the very slight difference in the margin of profit between first- and second-class species of fish hardly makes worthwhile the longer time required to catch first-class species. Furthermore, the competition from first-class fresh-water species from the São Francisco River during this time of year has serious effects on the Guaiamu market.

The third distinct season coincides with the forty-day Lenten period. In March and April the winds from the south and the southeast pick up slightly, and the winter season begins. Fishing, mostly for second-class species of fish is carried on well within the safety of the inner reef. The great demand for fish during the Lenten period, however, does encourage some fishermen to sail farther out in search of first-class species.

COGNITION AND THE CATCH

The fishermen of Coqueiral share a generalized knowledge of the area of the sea and the aspect of the land which comprise their fishing universe. The possibility of maximizing individual production rests on the fishermen's ability to locate particular species of fish according to their market values in different seasons. Toward this end, they have elaborated a complex system of named fishing grounds and landmarks.[3] The location of the fishing grounds by visual triangulation and knowledge of the distribution of fish within them in given seasons is transmitted over generations. This allows an increasing number of independent producers to locate fishing grounds, thereby maximizing the productive potential of the community. At the same time, secrecy regarding particular spots within the grounds serves as a spacing mechanism, which minimizes competition and prevents overfishing by according temporary property rights to individual fishermen.

Coqueiral's fishing boundaries extend along approximately twenty miles of coastline, from the village of Jitaí in the north to Joro in the south, and out some twenty miles to the edge of the continental shelf. The area includes those features of the landscape which are distinguishable from the ocean out to this limit. Distance is expressed either in terms of the ocean depth or the sailing time to a given spot, and rarely in terms of geographical or nautical miles.

It is within these boundaries that the fishing economy of Coqueiral operates. Beyond the edge of the continental shelf is another world, which belongs to the monsters of the sea and to the ships that sail past. It is a world entirely unknown to the fishermen of Coqueiral, and the captain who takes his jangada beyond the 200-fathom mark is said to be "tempting the devil."

Within their own world of fishing, however, the jangadeiros of Coqueiral have discovered and learned, and they have ordered their knowledge on several levels. This process is evident in the mapping out of smaller divisions within the total fishing area. The area of ocean plied by the jangadas from Coqueiral first is divided into named zones. Each zone runs perpendicular to the shoreline for one or two miles, and then out to the edge of the continental shelf. The name for each of these zones (Gurujú, Les-Nordeste, etc.) is taken from the particular area of land on which it fronts. Between the outer reef, which lies some ten miles offshore, and the edge of the continental shelf, individual zones are divided further into discrete sections, or fishing grounds. These subdivisions are made on the basis of depth and composition of the bottom, and they are named: *restinga, razinho, razo grande, razo,* and *parede,* this last being the edge of the continental shelf. Each major zone of the sea is separated by an area called a *liso,* which is comprised of a plain, sandy bottom that yields few, if any, fish. Such zoning creates a mosaic-like pattern, with a multiplicity and some duplication of named fishing grounds.[4] These grounds are identified by their own (land) names added to the name of the sea zone in which they are located (e.g., *raso do mar do Gurujú*).

Particular fishing spots are located within these fishing grounds. They may be jutting rocks, stretches of identifiable reefs, or submerged rocky areas which are frequented by fishermen because they have yielded good catches in the past. All fishing spots are marked and remembered by individual fishermen using a visual system of triangulation, which utilizes a series of landmarks that can be seen on clear days from most of Coqueiral's fishing grounds. The two commonly used landmarks are the mountain called Barriga, in the hinterland some twenty leagues to the north, and the Pacatuba range, in the state of Sergipe to the south. Of the two, the northern landmarks are more readily sited since the size and proximity of Barriga makes it visible from all of the northern fishing grounds. The distance of Pacatuba, on the other hand, puts it out of the visual range of most fishing grounds north of the zone called Les-Nordeste. In addition, the low, sandy coastal plain approaching the São Francisco River presents no second reference point that can be used for *marcação*, or "lining up."

All sorts of landmarks are used: a grove of coconut palms, a high sand dune, the outline of a familiar plantation, or the steeple of the Guaiamu Church. A fisherman is able to determine his course by "lining up" one landmark behind another in such a way as to constitute directional cues. Thus, to sail to the zone of Barreira do Velho, the steeple of the Guaiamu Church must appear about one arm's length from the Coqueiral dunes. The combination of two such landmarks into sets serves to guide a raft to a given fishing ground. Thus, when the steeple moves to the northeast of the village and nears the house of Dr. Fulano, and Barriga appears to touch on the Barra de Jitaí, a fisherman drops anchor at the edge of the continental shelf in the sea of Barreira do Velho.

Two well-spaced sets of landmarks are used simultaneously to fix a distinct fishing spot. The *marca de confrontação* is directly on the shore facing the raft. The *marca de altura* is at some distance away on a northern or southern shore. For example, one fisherman knows he has arrived at his favorite fishing spot when the Guaiamu steeple meets the "slippery hillside" (*marca de confrontação*) and the hillock of Pomba comes to rest between the second and third hillsides behind Piuma (*marca de altura*). Another favorite spot for first-class species of fish is where the Aves do Caboclo da Lagôa Azêda appears to touch on a hillock in Jacarecica (*marca de altura*) while a plantation angles in on Jitaí Lagoon, with a small coconut grove showing between them (*marca de confrontação*).

When fishing grounds are farther out, past the visual range of such landmarks, the fisherman takes his initial directional cues from the visible landmarks. As soon as he loses sight of these, however, he navigates by judging time and distance in accordance with prevailing winds. In the sea zone called Onça, for example, a fisherman loses sight of land after the fifty-meter mark. He then continues along the same course until he approximates the fishing ground, which lies between two *lisos*, or plain, sandy areas. Next he drops a plumb line to test the bottom. When the plumb line is recovered it is scrutinized and smelled in order to detect the composition of the bottom, and thereby to identify the location. Rocky areas are said to smell sweet, while gravel supposedly has a bad odor, and mud smells foul.

It is difficult to assess to what degree sets of landmarks are accurate in placing a raft exactly on the spot previously fished.[5] Fishermen say that if a rocky area is very small they may not be able to locate it again, even on the basis of landmarks. It is probable that landmarks do not put a jangada on the exact spot fished previously, but are more accurate than plumbing in guiding a raft to a similar spot within a general area of a fishing ground. In these areas, fish are not bound to a specific spot, and neither is effective production. Rather, it would seem that sets of landmarks bring a fisherman within certain fishing grounds where particular species of fish are caught.

The fishermen of Coqueiral conceive of the distribution of fish within fishing grounds not as a random process, but rather as a function of specific conditions, namely, depth and composition of the bottom. Depth is always expressed in terms of *braças* (2.2 meters), which are measured by drawing a length of fishing line across outstretched arms. The composition of the bottom refers to the general configuration of the ocean floor, whether rock, sand, gravel, or mud. Species of fish are classified according to their market values and located in particular settings.[6] Two distinct fishing patterns prevail. *Peixes de pedra*, or rock-living species with the highest commercial value, are generally caught in deeper waters beyond the fifty-meter mark. Second-class species are primarily caught closer to shore, within the ten-mile outer reef above gravel or mud bottoms.

While the jangadeiro is not fully aware of the entire range of phenomena which confronts him, he deduces much about certain aspects of his fishing universe. As a rule his knowledge is connected with the fishing strategy he himself employs, whether fishing for second-class species on the inner grounds or marking spots on the outer grounds for better qualities of fish. He expresses his knowledge in the idiom of a folk understanding of marine ecology.

Kottak (1966:227) has questioned the utility of a system of distinct fishing spots. He notes, correctly, that much of the fishing (in Arembepe) depends not on the demarcation of small fishing spots but on large zones. However, in my opinion, the importance of fishing

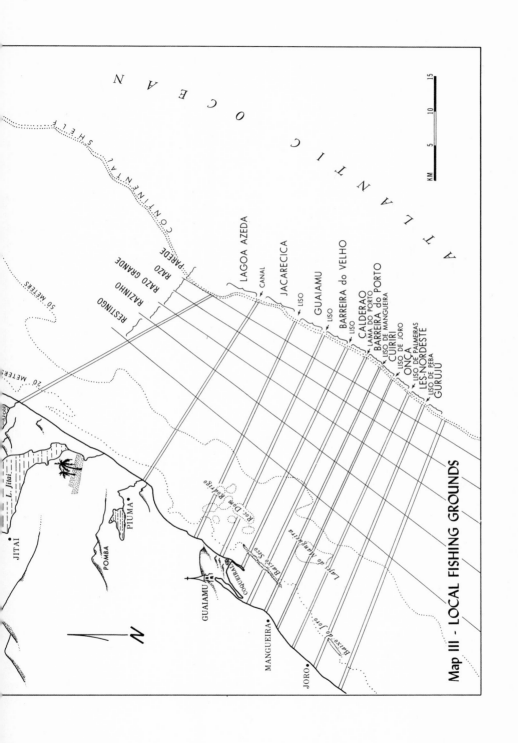

Map III - LOCAL FISHING GROUNDS

spots is not related to the entire fishing operation, but rather is a function of the species of fish being pursued. The marking of specific spots is not necessary for large shoals of fish, which travel in mid-water during certain seasons of the year, although it does become necessary for locating more "sedentary" species, which move about singly feeding on the smaller fish that hover around rocks.[7] The system of marked fishing spots in Coqueiral concerns itself only with rock-living species inhabiting the fishing grounds beyond the fifty-meter mark.

Kottak (1966:216–17) states that several attributes reminiscent of the "Protestant ethic" are far more important in determining differential success in fishing than familiarity with fishing spots. Youth, good health, sobriety, willingness to take calculated risks, and the ability to command allegiance of a crew are undoubtedly characteristics of successful fishermen. However, the information passed on through the system of named fishing grounds and landmarks is essential to becoming an independent producer in Coqueiral. The ability to locate given species of fish within different seasons is necessary if a fisherman is going to learn to distinguish between alternative fishing patterns and fish independently.

Kottak further states (1966:217) that beyond any utilitarian function the knowledge of fishing spots might have, it is a mechanism by which captains are differentiated from ordinary seamen and justifies their receiving a greater share of the catch. In Coqueiral, however, captains do not receive a greater share of the catch than ordinary fishermen. Moreover, captaincy is, at best, temporary, since it is a social category rather than an occupational grouping. All those who serve as captains on other people's rafts want to be independent producers, and most manage to fish on their own rafts during at least part of the year.

The art of "lining up" a specific spot is required, then, if a fisherman is to become an independent producer on his own log raft. Lining up requires an acute sense of vision, the loss of which often forces a fisherman to retire or accept a permanent position as a member of a crew.[8] Most fishermen are able to see land from most points on Coqueiral's fishing grounds, but not everyone can see it in the necessary detail. Moreover, and possibly more important, a fisherman must be able to account for winds and currents in judging the drift not only of his raft, but also of his lines. Finally, he must possess a keen memory in order to keep the fishing spots in his head. It takes time and practice to master this art,[9] which serves, in part, as a mechanism for guaranteeing a temporary crew in a situation where everyone wants to be an independent producer.

Fishermen speak openly about the fishing grounds, the names used for them, and the seasonal movement of fish within them. The fishing grounds are, thus, common knowledge among all the raft fishermen of Coqueiral. There is, however, very little discussion regarding specific fishing spots which can be marked, and which are held to be far better than others because of their alleged constant yield. These remain the private reserves of those fishermen capable of sailing to them. Individual differences exist, therefore, only in terms of the specific fishing spots exploited by particular fishermen, who give them special descriptive names reflecting the set of markings which are used in sailing to them. The fact that all fishermen do not know how to go to a given area is a function of individual ability to mark and remember locations. Secrecy accounts for the fact that some fishermen know fewer spots than others.

A fisherman rarely teaches the art of lining up a specific fishing spot, and a boy's apprenticeship consists largely of curiosity and persistence. While a fisherman is always delighted to have a young apprentice to help augment his catch, he avoids taking him to a preferred spot. When pursuing species of fish of better quality, a crew is not told to what spot they are sailing until they are well out of the harbor.

The zealous guarding of spots as secrets and the attempts of others to find them are constant causes of contention in Coqueiral. Sometimes a fisherman will even follow a raft, whereupon its captain is likely to lift anchor and sail off in anger to avoid revealing his favorite fishing spot. In one of many instances, two brothers-in-law ceased to speak when one revealed the location of a spot which the other had entrusted to him. At the same time, social factors implement the maintenance of secrecy by awarding prestige to the captain who knows many spots and does not divulge them. In a sense, this has an economic basis, since captains are rated according to the size of their catches, and it is the best captain who knows the most fishing spots.

What then is the function of this secrecy? It does not serve to keep the art of lining up in the hands of a privileged class (Kottak

1966:163). The entire range of shared knowledge of the fishing grounds and landmarks would seem to preclude this possibility. An enterprising fisherman can follow the navigational cues, and once on the fishing spot he has only to look to shore and see how the landmarks fit together.

It is my view that secrecy functions as an ecologically adaptive mechanism with regard to certain aspects of the total fishing operation. It must be remembered that not all aspects of fishing demand the location of specific spots and that not all spots are guarded secrets. In some instances, a fisherman will signal another with a wave of a hat if a particular species of fish is plentiful and is biting. This, however, occurs only on grounds in which second-class species of fish appear in shoals, grounds which are close enough to be seen from shore and are thus available to all fishermen. On these occasions, a spacing mechanism operates so that lines will not get tangled and fishermen will not interfere with each other's productivity. By the same token, spots beyond the fifty-meter mark in the southern waters, which cannot be marked, are not as avowedly secret as others. Since a fisherman has a plumb and cannot mark the spot visually, he can only approximate the area fished and cannot locate it as precisely. Plumbing, therefore, serves as a natural process of randomization of fishing spots in lieu of the social mechanism of secrecy.

It is fishing on the outer grounds for the most valued species in areas which can be localized by landmarks that is characterized by the greatest amount of secrecy. Very little information is vouchsafed regarding specific fishing spots, which can be marked, and which are held to be far better than others because of their allegedly constant yield. These remain the private reserves of fishermen capable of sailing to them. According to Bottomanne (1959:128):

The more vessels are amassed, the more they influence each other's catches and the more the acceleration of the decreasing catches per unit is felt . . . smart skippers often try to find their own places. In such cases, the temporary "sole ownership" of *even mediocre* [emphasis mine] fishing grounds may sometimes prove a better source of earnings than the fishing of mass-exploited grounds.

The most constant characteristic of all fisheries is common ownership of the resources of the sea (Bottomanne 1959:8). However, this is also one of its chief dilemmas (Gordon 1954:125). In Coqueiral, ready access to the sea on small log rafts is highly conducive to entry into the fishing economy, particularly since the distribution of agricultural land is sharply limited. Jangada fishing is a reliable means of subsistence for a large number of independent peasant producers. Approximately one hundred different rafts ply the waters around Coqueiral at various times during the year.[10] Yet the lack of motors, of scientific navigational instruments, and of storage and sleeping facilities seriously limits the distance to which they might otherwise sail. All fishing is done above the continental shelf, and the size and weight of the catch is thereby restricted. Fishing grounds around Coqueiral are limited in extent, and fish populations do not afford an unlimited source of supply despite their reproductive capacities (Bottomanne 1959:8; Gordon 1954:125; Wynne-Edwards 1962:4).[11] Only about two hundred square miles of ocean are accessible in which the fishermen of Coqueiral can catch first-class species of fish, and the number of good spots within this area is sharply reduced by the small number of favorable fishing banks.[12] A general increase in fishing intensity could lead to a general decrease in yield per individual fishing unit once the optimum level of production has been reached (Bottomanne 1959:8; Russell 1942:75; Wynne-Edwards 1962:5). While overfishing is perhaps unlikely, in view of the rudimentary techniques in use, the more vessels there are fishing on the relatively few good fishing spots, the less the efficiency of each vessel. Increased demands on the food supply and the intensification of the quest invite the danger of uncontrolled competition and, thereby, the eventual depletion of certain first-class species of fish which already are in short supply.

Any economic activity thus affected by the law of diminishing returns[13] requires a mechanism for conserving the stock, which would maintain both the total productive capacity of the community and the maximum efficiency of individual units up to a point. To go beyond that point would result in overexploitation and prove to the lasting detriment of the fishermen themselves. Any decrease in the productive efficiency of peasant producers, who already function with a very small margin of profit, would probably decrease their earnings below the cost of operation and put them out of business. We can assume, therefore, that independent production in Coqueiral is held at least at a constant level. We can hypothesize that the mechanism which maintains steady production can be found in the elaborate system of spacing that is based on named fishing grounds and landmarks, by which the fishermen of Coqueiral conduct their daily work. Secrecy of fishing spots within these grounds serves to minimize competition by affording temporary property rights to individual fishermen. The massing of rafts on particular fishing spots would certainly decrease the size of the catch for each unit, and competition would compel a fisherman to return frequently and early to a favorite fishing spot, which might otherwise be fished out by someone else. Furthermore, there is evidence indicating that where ownership of fishing equipment has become concentrated in the hands of single companies or a few individuals, the phenomenon of secrecy disappears and resources are depleted (see Chapter I).

PRODUCTION

Despite their generalized knowledge of marine ecology, production among jangadeiros in Coqueiral is curtailed by the primitive methods still in use. Hook-and-line fishing from log rafts, because it is subject to the seasonal and daily migrations of fish and to the vagaries of weather conditions, seriously limits the production at sea. Oar- and sail-driven rafts require an enormous number of man-hours for the often dangerous passage to and from the fishing grounds, which on occasion approximates or even surpasses the time actually spent fishing. While catches up to 300 kilos were reported for a *jangada de alto*, the largest single catch of fish during my stay in the village was a shark weighing 90 kilos.

The catch of fresh fish on all jangadas is stored in the *samburá*, or basket, which is kept under the salting platform. On rare occasions, a fish so large that it can be carried on the floor of a raft without being washed overboard is wedged under the salting platform. Catches of fresh fish are normally limited to the size of the *samburá*, however, and once it has been filled the jangada returns to shore. Salted catches are carried on the *salgadeira*, where they are protected from the action of waves that constantly wash over the logs. Fishermen prefer not to salt fish, except when sailing time and distance make it essential, since the salting process takes time away from fishing, and the Cr$100 ($.06) per kilo increase in price which they are allowed for salted fish does not compensate them for the additional outlay in both time and material.

A comparison of production for each of the different types of rafts during the principal fishing seasons reveals the nature of the alternative fishing strategies (see Table 9). Production records were kept for *jangadas de alto, paquetes, botes à vela*, and *botes de remo* over two thirty-day periods, one during the winter season (July to August), and the other at the very beginning of the summer fishing season (September to October). Data was collected on crew members, sailing time, actual time spent fishing, grounds exploited, and quantity and type of fish caught and sold. The four data sheets chosen for comparison were selected from among those taken for some twenty rafts because of the completeness of the record in these four cases, and also because of their apparent typicality.

Jangada de Alto

In the thirty-day winter period, July 10 to August 10, the *jangada de alto* fished with a two-man crew for thirteen days, or a total of eighty-six man-hours per fisherman. An additional forty-two hours were spent sailing to and from the fishing grounds. On three particular days, the trip by raft to and from a rocky fishing area some fifteen miles out to sea took about five hours, and an average of ten hours' fishing was done each day. During these three days, the crew caught 54 kilos of first-class fish, 40 kilos of which were sold for Cr$16,0000 ($8.80). One day, at a distance of nine miles from shore, 13 kilos of first-class fish were caught in a period of three hours. Ten kilos of these fish were sold for Cr$4,000 ($2.20). On the nine other days, the raft fished three miles out for second-class species. Sailing time averaged three hours, and approximately six hours per day were spent in fishing. A total of 146 kilos were caught, 110 kilos of which were sold for Cr$33,000 ($18). Not once during this period did the raft stay out overnight. The average daily catch totaled 16.3 kilos, and the total earnings for the month for this one raft were Cr$53,000 ($29).

The same *jangada de alto* spent sixteen days at sea in the thirty-day period from September 24 to October 24, 1965. On only fourteen of the sixteen days was any catch brought in at all. A total of 126 man-hours

TABLE 9. PRODUCTION STATISTICS FOR SAMPLE ONE-MONTH PERIODS OF FOUR RAFTS IN COQUEIRAL

	JANGADA		PAQUETE		BOTE À VELA		BOTE DE REMO	
	winter	summer	winter	summer	winter	summer	winter	summer
Days at sea	13	16	16	14	18	24	18	19
Days with recorded catch	13	14	16	13	17	23	17	19
Hours under sail	42	60	46	55	46	55	55	54
Hours fishing	86	126	79	59	87	92	91	79
Days seeking 1st-class fish	4	3	4	6				
Average hours under sail	5	6	5.5	4				
Average hours fishing	10	10	4.5	4				
Total kilos caught	67	14	33	23.5				
Kilos sold	50	10	24	18				
Earnings	Cr$20,000 ($11)	Cr$4,000 ($2.20)	Cr$9,600 ($5.30)	Cr$7,200 ($4)				
Days seeking 2nd-class fish	9	13	12	8	18	24	18	18
Average hours under sail	3	3	3.5	2.5	2.5	2	3	2.8
Average hours fishing	6	6	5	4	5	3.8	5	4
Total kilos caught	146	155	95	67	67	107	52	61
Kilos sold	110	103	69	51	47	70	29	36
Earnings	Cr$33,000 ($18)	Cr$30,900 ($17)	Cr$20,700 ($11)	Cr$15,300 ($8.50)	Cr$14,100 ($7.80)	Cr$21,000 ($12)	Cr$8,700 ($5)	Cr$10,800 ($6)
Days seeking 3rd-class fish								
Total kilos caught				23.5				
Kilos sold				17				
Earnings				Cr$3,400 ($1.30)				
Total monthly earnings	Cr$53,000 ($29)	Cr$34,900 ($19.20)	Cr$30,300 ($16.30)	Cr$25,900 ($13.80)	Cr$14,100 ($7.80)	Cr$21,000 ($12)	Cr$8,700 ($5)	Cr$10,800 ($6)

per fisherman was spent fishing, while some sixty additional hours were spent under sail. On three days the raft went after first-class species, averaging six-hours' sailing time to and from the fishing grounds, which are about twenty-one miles out to sea. Some ten hours per day were spent in actual fishing. On the first of these three days, 14 kilos of first-class fish were caught, 10 kilos of which were sold for Cr$4,000 ($2.20). On the two subsequent days, however, the fishermen's luck failed, and no fish were caught at the same fishing spot. Thirteen days were spent approximately six miles offshore, fishing for second-class species. An average of six hours per day was spent fishing, and three additional hours were spent under sail. On these days, 155 kilos of second-class fish were caught, and 103 kilos were sold for Cr$30,900 ($17). The average daily catch for the summer month decreased to 10.5 kilos, while the monthly earnings came to only Cr$34,900 ($19.20), owing primarily to the two unsuccessful days spent in search of first-class species.

Paquete

In the winter period, the *paquete* fished sixteen days with success. A two-man crew accumulated seventy-nine man-hours per fisherman of fishing and an additional total of forty-six hours under sail. Four of these days were spent some twelve miles out in search of first-class species. An average of four hours per day was spent sailing, while only five and one-half hours per day of fishing were recorded during the period. A total of 33 kilos of fish was caught, out of which 24 kilos were sold for Cr$9,600 ($5.30). Twelve days during this period were spent fishing above gravel and mud bottoms some six to seven miles offshore. Sailing time on these days averaged three and one-half to four hours, and the average daily fishing time was four hours and forty minutes. A total of 95 kilos of fish was caught, and 69 of these were sold for Cr$20,700 ($11). The *paquete* averaged 8 kilos per day, or less than one-half the average daily catch of the *jangada de alto* for the same period. It also fished for approximately half the time. The total monthly earnings for the raft were only Cr$30,300 ($16.30).

In the summer period, the same *paquete* fished fourteen days, thirteen of them successfully, for a total of fifty-nine man-hours per fisherman. An additional fifty-five hours were spent sailing to and from the fishing grounds. On six of these days, the raft sailed out some fifteen miles to the rocky fishing grounds for first-class species of fish, averaging four hours sailing to the spots and five hours fishing per day. Again, the *paquete* spent only about one-half as many hours fishing as the *jangada de alto*. Forty-seven kilos of fish were caught, but only one-half were of first-class variety. On three days, only third-class species of fish were caught. These weighed a total of 23.5 kilos, 17 kilos of which sold for only Cr$3,400 ($1.30). Eighteen kilos of first-class catch sold for Cr$7,200 ($4). Eight days were spent fishing for second-class species at the outer reefs some nine miles offshore. The average was two and one-half hours in sailing time and four hours in fishing time per day, in this case one-third less time than the *jangada de alto*. On one day the fishermen caught nothing. The total catch for these eight days came to 67 kilos, 51 of which were sold for Cr$15,300 ($8.50). The average catch per day was 8.1 kilos, only 2.4 kilos below the *jangada de alto* for the same period, despite a considerable reduction in the number of man-hours expended in fishing. The total monthly earnings for the raft were Cr$25,900 ($13.80).

Bote à Vela

A *bote à vela* with only one man aboard spent eighteen days at sea in the winter months. On each of seventeen days a catch was brought to shore. All fishing for second-class species was done approximately six miles out, just behind the inner reef, on a gravel bottom. The average fishing time was slightly above five hours per day, while the sailing time to and from the spots averaged only two and one-half hours per day. A total of 67 kilos was caught, and 47 of these were sold for Cr$14,100 ($7.80). The average catch per day was 4.7 kilos, or more than half the amount caught on the two-man *paquete* for the same period.

In the month during summer the same *bote à vela* sailed on twenty-four days and brought in catches on twenty-three days. The lone fisherman spent a total of ninety-two hours fishing and an additional fifty-five hours under sail. All fishing was done within a three-mile limit, with an occasional foray out to the inner reefs, located five miles from shore. Sailing time averaged slightly over two hours per day, while an average of three hours and forty-eight minutes per day was spent fishing. A total of 107 kilos of fish was caught; 70 of these were sold for Cr$21,000 ($12). The average catch per day was 4.5 kilos.

Bote de Remo

One man fished from the *bote de remo* for a total of eighteen days during the thirty-day winter period. Fish were caught on seventeen of these days. A total of ninety-one man-hours was spent fishing, and fifty-five hours were spent rowing to the nearby grounds. All fishing for second-class species was done on gravel bottom, well within a limit of three miles offshore. The average fishing time per day was five hours, and the time spent rowing to and from the fishing grounds averaged three hours. A total of 52 kilos of fish was caught, 29 kilos of which sold for Cr$8,700 ($5). The average catch per day was a mere 2.8 kilos.

At the beginning of the summer period, the same fisherman began to row out to the grounds just behind the inshore reef along the east coast of the village. A total of nineteen days and nineteen catches was recorded. Seventy-nine man-hours were expended in rowing out to the spot and back again. No lack of winds nor prohibitive currents ever made it necessary to leave the raft on one of the northern beaches. The average fishing time per day was four hours, while an average of two hours and forty-eight minutes per day was spent rowing. A total of 61 kilos of fish was caught, 36 kilos of which sold for Cr$10,800 ($6). The average catch per day was 3.2 kilos.

The comparative data indicates that large, sail-driven jangadas consistently catch more fish regardless of the season. Still, this margin of profit amounts to only a few hundred kilos, which must then be divided among the crew. One successful casting of a large beach seine provides its owner with a catch larger than that from a month's fishing on a jangada. The production of larger rafts decreases in the summer, even though more second-class species of fish are caught, because the total weight per catch is not as great as that yielded when larger-sized first-class species are caught in small numbers. In the case of smaller rafts, the catch is increased in the summer months, when fishermen are able to sail out alone after abundant second-class species of fish. While the catch on a *bote* amounts to only about a hundred kilos per raft, it does not have to be shared.

Jangadeiros choose between fishing as a member of a crew and fishing independently by calculating individual earnings and not the total earnings of the productive unit. Independent producers earn more in the summer months than members of jangada crews. The system of redistribution and of marketing has far-reaching effects on individual earnings, and a consideration of these factors is essential to an understanding of the choices that fishermen make between alternative fishing strategies.

[VI]

Distribution and Redistribution

THE FACTORS involved in making an economic choice between fishing independently and fishing as a member of a crew cannot be stated merely in terms of comparative costs and earnings. The advantages and disadvantages of alternative fishing strategies are not apparent from an examination of production data alone. In a market economy, the entire system of redistribution has an important effect upon earnings.[1] The division of the catch, its distribution through middlemen, and the reactions and trends of the market are all factors essential to an understanding of the choices made between the available means of production.

The villagers of Coqueiral can recognize jangadas several miles out at sea, and there are always a number of interested parties waiting to help beach a raft on its return from a day's fishing. These include the sons and wives of the jangadeiros themselves, the vendors who buy from them, and the beggars who help to push the raft on shore in the hope that the day's catch will provide some small fish in return. All of them share in some way in the direct redistribution of fish among the participants in the productive unit and in the marketing of fish in the hinterland. The few nonfishing owners of some of the rafts, who make fishing an entrepreneurial activity, also appear on the beach. They come to inspect the catch and to supervise at the weigh-in scale.

After the raft has been pushed out of reach of the incoming tide by means of rollers made from coconut tree trunks, the fishing tackle is removed and the division of the catch begins. Wives and children take the fish set aside for home consumption, and the fish hawkers carry the rest to the weigh-in scale. Fish for sale is always weighed in the presence of the fisherman or a representative of his household. Each fisherman sells his catch independently, since he receives his share in fish, never in money.

There are several ways in which the catch is shared among the fishermen belonging to a productive unit. The most common is the system of *meiação*, in which the owner of the raft, whether a participant fisherman or not, takes half the catch of each member of his crew. First, approximately 20% to 30% of the catch is divided into a number of small equal shares, one for each of the crew members and the owner. This percentage always is estimated on the total number rather than the weight of fish and is set aside for home consumption. A nonfishing owner receives half of the remaining catch, the other half being divided equally among the members of the crew. When an owner fishes on his own raft, whether as captain or crew member, he marks the fish he hooked himself, thereby retaining all of his own catch and still taking a half from the crew. In a crew made up of three fishermen, the owner-captain fishes "separate line" *(linha separada)*, while the two crew members fish "joint line" *(linha junta)* and share half of their catch with the owner. In no instance does a captain receive a regular gratuity from the owner either in cash payments or on a percentage of the fish caught. Some captains who take care of the rafts from which they fish occasionally get an additional token gift of fish.

At times fishermen deliberately catch for sale on the market species that are generally used as bait. On these occasions the system of *meiação* prevails. However, when the same species are caught on a trawl line for use as bait, but are not used as such and instead are brought to shore for sale, the division of the catch is in thirds. One share goes to the captain, one to the crew, and one to the owner. The nonowner captain also receives his part of the crew's share. All fish caught for sale on a trawl line are divided up in this way, whether or not the captain is also the owner. The amount of fish caught by trawling was not determined, and therefore it was difficult to judge if such catches are of commercial significance or if they serve as substantial gratuities for the nonowner captain. The prime species, *cavala (Scomber colias)*, or Spanish mackerel, which is caught while trawling, brings the best market price and provides the captain with the incentive to keep a trawl line tied on to his thigh while he maneuvers the raft out toward the fishing grounds. As previously mentioned, the use of *cavala* for bait in spite of its high value reflects the limited market for first-class fish and also the lack of effective techniques for preserving this highly perishable species.

If an owner loans a raft with neither food nor fishing tackle, the division of the catch is in three parts, one as payment for the loan of the raft and two divided among the crew. In such cases, the owner does not remove any fish to cover the cost of food, and his share of the catch is equal to that of each crew member. When an owner supplies food and equipment along with the loan of a raft, the division of the catch follows the standard system of *meiação*. In all cases in which the catch is divided into three parts, a share of the catch, estimated to cover the owner's cost of food and other operating costs related to sustenance of the crew and preservation of the catch, is deducted first

The general arrangement among kinsmen who fish together is also that of *meiação*. In cases where two kinsmen fish together and a third nonkin crew member goes along, it is normally the latter who marks his catch and contributes half to the earnings of the kinsmen. Under certain circumstances, as in the case of retired fishermen who have bought rafts for younger kinsmen, the owner may take merely a quantity of fish to eat. In cases where kinsmen are from one household, no division of the catch is made and earnings revert to the senior member. When the kinsmen represent two households, the degree of the relationship and the needs of the households determine the amount of sharing that is done. In cases where nonfishing owners use rafts for commercial ventures, the strict rules of *meiação* apply, whether or not the captain is a kinsman, and the arrangements are on a strictly business basis.

The share system is the only means by which possible financial ruin can be averted by small owners who otherwise could not afford to pay wages on days when fishing is poor. Perhaps it also serves to maintain the incentive of crews that are not generally supervised in their work. The advantages of this system for the owner of a large raft are obvious. Still, as we shall see, the disadvantages to crew members are numerous, and for this reason fishermen prefer to fish on their own small rafts as independent producers. These disadvantages also explain why many jangadeiros alternate between crews in the winter months and independent production in the summer season. Before discussing the patterns of ownership and crew composition, however, it is necessary to give an idea of differential earnings on the rafts.

Most of the fish caught are weighed at a scale operated by the Colônia de Pescadores that is housed in the center of the beach, where it is within clear view of the entire bay. When jangadas are out at night, a kerosene lamp is left burning at the weigh-in scale to remind fishermen of their obligations. Oftentimes fishermen and their hawkers will neglect to awaken the tax collector and instead will weigh the fish on one of the small, privately-owned scales in the village. Although the directors of the fishermen's guild strongly deny the fact of "contraband" fish, it is to both the fishermen's and the fish hawkers' advantage to avoid paying taxes from which no benefits are forthcoming.

Money rarely changes hands at the weigh-in scale. The tax collector notes the weight of the fish, and he then calculates the 10% due the Colônia de Pescadores, and the Cr$2 per kilo which accrue to the county from the taxes levied on the fishermen and the fish hawkers, respectively. Both the tax collector and the fishermen receive payment after the fish have been retailed.

There is almost no retail buying on the beach, unless it is done through a fish hawker. Although consumers often help to beach a jangada in the hope of buying some fish at wholesale prices from a sympathetic jangadeiro, convention requires that fishermen sell through vendors. The fishermen actually prefer to deal through such middlemen since price controls preclude earning additional money through the direct sale of fish on the beach. Furthermore, the work of beaching a jangada and dividing the catch would be complicated if a fisherman had to account for both the fish and the receipt of cash.

Relations between fishermen and consumers have long been strained because retail buyers often try to purchase even the small portion of fish that a fisherman has set aside for home consumption. Fishermen are extremely sensitive to these pressures, and most tend to recall a nineteenth-century attempt at armed reprisal against the jangadeiros in Coqueiral who refused to sell their catch to soldiers from the county seat.[2] While fishermen prefer not to sell to consumers on the beach, many of them would like the additional income that retail prices afford. Both the mayor's office and the fishermen's guild, however, prohibit a fisherman from assuming the additional role of middleman, and thus from earning the difference between wholesale and retail prices. Sr. Nilo, the president of the fishermen's guild, stated that it would be "unfair for a fisherman to earn two profits."

The fishermen sell independently to fish hawkers, or *pombeiros*, and the owner of a raft cannot insist that crew members sell in consort to one buyer. The alternation of fishing strategies between sailing as part of a crew and independent production supports the individual selection of fish hawkers. In April, 1965, there were twenty-one fish hawkers in Coqueiral, eleven of them males and ten, females. Of the eleven males, only six had regular customers among the fishermen. One man bought fish regularly, but he bought it from other hawkers for resale in the hinterland. The four other hawkers bought fish only on those occasions when fishermen without regular buyers had a large enough catch to sell.

All of the *pombeiros* buy from a limited number of fishermen, and some buy only from a single relative. Although sixty-four of the eighty-five regular fishermen in Coqueiral have their own *pombeiros*, no single hawker has more than eight suppliers. Most hawkers buy from only four or five fishermen. Although the hawker with the largest number of suppliers also owns two rafts that he operates on a share system, his crew do not sell him their share of the catch. He does hawk his owner's share, however.

A hawker-fisherman relationship, once established, is accompanied by a distinct set of obligations. *Pombeiros* must buy whatever fish their suppliers care to sell. Failure to do so results in the loss of that particular supplier and probably of others. Hawkers are also expected to pay their suppliers immediately upon their return from the market, and failure to do so can also mean loss of suppliers.

Fish hawkers, for their part, have a number of expectations with regard to the fishermen from whom they buy. They expect fishermen to retail fish only through a middleman. Moreover, they expect their suppliers to fish at every opportunity so that there will always be a steady supply of fish to market. One of the most common arguments among kinsmen concerns excess drinking, since drunkenness can prevent a fisherman from going to sea and can result in a loss of income for his entire family. Hawkers also expect that their kinsmen will sell them fish, and one often hears remarks such as "Look, he's my brother-in-law and he doesn't even sell me his catch!"

The large number of middlemen in Coqueiral is explained in part by the economic needs of the extended family. While fishermen are unable to retail fish themselves, they sometimes sell through a kinsman and thereby add to their own household income. This is the case in three households in which the husbands and sons sell to resident female hawkers. In most instances in which a fisherman sells to a kinsman, however, he is acting to help a relative who is in need. Thus, a pregnant woman prepares for the cost of childbirth by selling fish while she is able. In one case, a father and son who fish on the same raft and reside in the same household sell their fish separately to the father's two sisters, despite the fact that all earnings revert to the father. As in cases involving kinsmen in the same productive unit, no money changes hands when members of a single household are involved in a buyer-client relationship. When kinsmen from different households are involved, however, the same rules of exchange that apply in financial dealings with nonkinsmen are followed.

Kin obligations are not directed toward women only. Young men often are financed in a first market venture. Of the six male *pombeiros* with regular suppliers, five started their careers as hawkers while still young men, on the encouragement of kinsmen who financed their initial venture. Two of these men are now established hawkers who buy exclusively from kinsmen. Three others are related in some degree to at least half of their suppliers. The fifth hawker is a newcomer to the village, and none of his five suppliers is a kinsman.

Of the ten women hawkers in the village, four buy fish exclusively from kinsmen, and three others report that more than half of their suppliers are relatives. Three female hawkers have no relatives among their suppliers. Two of these are unmarried women, and none of the three has fishermen living in her household.

Fishermen claim to prefer male fish hawkers to females since men can handle more fish and allegedly have more fluid cash. They contend that women buy exclusively on credit and that they cannot handle large catches. Nevertheless, there are as many women hawkers as males, and this cannot be explained on the basis of kin obligations alone. A larger proportion of male hawkers number kinsmen among their suppliers. Moreover, most of the female *pombeiros* are married and have income from resident males, so that they are not in particular need of extrafamilial support.

All of the female hawkers sell locally at the Guaiamu market. They carry the fish on their heads in a four-pound wooden tray called a *gamela*. Usually they must make several trips for more than 25 kilos of fish. In this way, a female hawker might be away from the beach when a fisherman arrives with his catch. One woman, when confronted with large catches, sends fish to market on her son's donkey.

For the most part, the men are able to carry more weight than the female hawkers, and one young vendor has taken up to 42 kilos in a *gamela* in one trip. However, four of the regular male *pombeiros* use mules to transport fish to market. Three of these men salt and store fish during the week for sale at the Sunday market at the sugar mill. A fourth *pombeiro* buys fish from other hawkers after the close of the Saturday market at Guaiamu and sells it still fresh on Sundays at the Palmeira agricultural colony.

Both wholesale and retail prices of fish are set by the president of the Colônia de Pescadores and by the mayor. The price of different classes of fish varies, but not according to laws of supply and demand. Price ceilings are set, and neither fishermen nor hawkers are permitted to earn more than the established margin of profit. At the same time, prices fall sharply when the supply of fish is especially abundant, since demand for fish remains essentially constant in the limited consumer market, and also because there is no way to satisfactorily conserve fish against future demand.

As Table 10 indicates, fish hawkers who sell in Guaiamu are permitted to earn only Cr$100 ($.06) per kilo of fish above the price paid to the fishermen on the beach and Cr$200 ($.12) per kilo for fish they salt themselves. Fishermen get Cr$100 ($.06) per kilo more for fish they salt at sea. Only Cr$100 ($.06) separates the price of first- and second-class species of fish, and there is a difference in price of only Cr$50 ($.03) between each of the other three classes. *Cavala (Scomber colias)*, or Spanish mackerel, is considered special and brings the highest wholesale and retail prices, selling on the beach at Coqueiral for Cr$500 ($.27) per kilo. Other first-class species sell for only Cr$400 ($.22) per kilo, the second-class species for Cr$300 ($.16) per kilo, and the third-class species for Cr$250 ($.13) per kilo.

Salted second-class fish sells at the same price as the fresh first-class species, and salted fish is always sold at inland markets where competition from preferred fresh fish is not a problem. The increased cost of salted fish, and its loss of flavor and of nutritive value, make it much less palatable to the landholding class which can afford to buy it. The difficulties of transportation and of preservation coincide with the mayor's demands that fresh fish be marketed only in the county capital. Hawkers defy the officials, and when they can, they sell fresh and salted fish on the beach or in Estrada Velha, the village lining the road between Coqueiral and Guaiamu. This relieves them of the burden of carrying the heavy load all the way to town. They also sell salted fish in bulk at reduced prices to vendors who carry it to inland markets.

None of the fish hawkers in Coqueiral is prepared to handle large quantities of fish, and they often lower their prices when abundant catches introduce a large financial risk. They prefer to sell out everything at once at a reduced margin of profit to someone who will salt the catch and carry it further into the interior, rather than risk not selling it at all. In the same way, fish bought after the close of the Saturday market in the county capital is sold at half of the established margin of profit to other hawkers from the village, who transport it by mule to the Sunday markets at the sugar mill or at the agricultural colony.

TABLE 10. WHOLESALE AND RETAIL PRICES OF FISH

	WHOLESALE		RETAIL	
CLASS	(Coqueiral)		(Guaiamu)	
	fresh	salted	fresh	salted
1	Cr$400	Cr$500	Cr$500	Cr$600
2	300	400	400	500
3	250	350	350	450
4	200	300	300	400
5	150	250	250	350

Hawkers from Coqueiral who sell salted fish at the Usina Bôa Fé or in Palmeira buy it at regular wholesale prices from the fishermen on the beach and at Cr$50 ($.03) per kilo more from fellow *pombeiros* who sell only in Guaiamu. They sell the same fish at a Cr$150–Cr$200 ($.09–$.12) per kilo increment in the valley, rather than at the Cr$100 ($.06) per kilo mark-up they would get at the county seat (see Table 10). Their margin of profit is increased even more when they sell fish which they salt themselves. For example, 5 kilos of fish require approximately 1 kilo of salt, which is bought at Cr$220 ($.12) per kilo.[3] The total cost of 5 kilos of salted first-class fish comes to Cr$2,220 ($1.20), not including the cost of labor involved in the salting process. The fish is sold at Cr$7,000 ($3.80) per kilo at the sugar mill or at the agricultural colony, yielding Cr$3,500 ($1.90), or at a profit of Cr$1,280 ($.71) for the 5 kilos. The hawker is thus earning Cr$256 ($.14) per kilo in profit, as opposed to the usual Cr$150–Cr$200 ($.09–$.12) for fish bought already processed.

The further inland one goes the greater the margin of profit. Hawkers who sell salted fish in the hinterland do not suffer from the competition of fresh fish nor from the restrictions on profits. Traders who come to Guaiamu from interior counties by truck to sell meat and *farinha* at the Saturday market often try to buy fish from the hawkers from Coqueiral. They buy fresh first-class fish at Cr$450 ($.25) per kilo and pre-salted first-class fish at Cr$550 ($.30) per kilo. They then truck the fish well into the hinterland, where it is sold for Cr$1,000 ($.55) per kilo or more. The margin of profit yielded is well worth the risk involved in the outlay of their earnings from the sale of goods in Guaiamu.

TABLE 11. WHOLESALE AND RETAIL PRICES OF FISH SOLD AT
USINA BOA FÉ AND PALMEIRA

CLASS OF FISH	WHOLESALE (Coqueiral)			RETAIL (Valley)		
	fresh	*(resale)*	*salted*	*(resale)*	*fresh*	*salted*
1	Cr$400	(+50)	500	(+50)	600	700
2	300	(+50)	400	(+50)	500	600
3	250	(+50)	350	(+50)	450	550

The earnings of the hawkers from Coqueiral who salt and store fish for sale in the valley are greater than those of the hawkers whose market is limited strictly to Guaiamu. There are, however, factors which cut into the profits of the former. In the first place, there is a loss of weight on fish that have been eviscerated before salting.[4] Secondly, the trip to the interior involves the additional expense of keep for a donkey and food for both the young boy who rides him and for the hawker himself. One hawker estimates his Sunday expenditure at approximately Cr$1,600 ($.88); to recompensate himself he needs to sell at least 6 kilos of fish. Finally, by speculating with larger quantities of fish over longer periods of time, these hawkers face a greater risk of loss than the hawkers who market small quantities of fresh fish in the county capital. The effectiveness of the salting process depends on the strength of the brining solution and the length of time the fish are treated. Local fish hawkers neither pack fish in salt nor use a heavy brine solution. They prefer to cut down on the expense of salt in the hope of selling fish quickly at the local market. Poorly salted fish keep only for a limited number of days in the tropics, however, and a failure to sell a week's store on Sunday can result in a total loss for the week.

The Guaiamu market is limited, especially for fresh fish, which must be sold within the immediate coastal zone before spoilage sets in. Even in the summer, when tourists take up residence on the beach at Coqueiral, there is only a slight increase in demand for first-class fish. Most of the twenty-three families who come to Coqueiral in the summer live in the valley all year round. Their patterns of consumption have little seasonal effect on the market situation, especially since fishing production is significantly increased in the summer months. Only in the Lenten period, when high-quality fish are not easily caught, does demand seem to exceed supply. But even at this time price ceilings hold earnings down, despite the increased demand.

In the summer season, production is increased by coastal fishing in Coqueiral, and the supply of fish is greatly augmented by the beach seines in Coqueiral and other coastal communities. Riverine fishing is also much expanded in the summer, and fresh-water fish of first-class variety from the São Francisco River flood the interior markets, competing with the catch from Coqueiral. The scarcity of fish during the Lenten period and for most of the winter season offers greater security to hawkers than the abundant supply during the summer months when the competition for the limited market is greatly increased.

The number of fish hawkers fluctuates with the season and the state of the market. During the height of the Lenten period, there were twenty-one fish hawkers in Coqueiral. The number decreased to seventeen in the winter season. It is significant that the decrease was in the number of the male hawkers and not among the females, which perhaps reflects the fact that kin obligations are felt more strongly toward women. In the winter season, many fishermen give half of their catch to the owner of a larger raft on which they are fishing, and therefore have little to sell to a hawker. Independent production in the summer, however, warrants a permanent buyer, and in the summer of 1964 the number of hawkers increased to twenty-five.

Since the catch per fisherman of second-class species of fish is smaller, losses that occur in the winter months are more easily sustained. Thus, one hawker claims to have lost Cr$60,000 ($33) in the catfish harvest of 1964. Another suffered losses of Cr$16,000 ($8.80), and a third, of Cr$6,000 ($3.30) during the same harvest. None of these losses was so great as to force the hawker into bankruptcy. When catches are extremely large, however, and prices fall, the fishermen stave off the hawkers' financial ruin by lowering the established wholesale price and sustaining a far smaller margin of profit. Thus, one hawker bought 200 kilos of fish from his client and was able to sell it at only Cr$210 ($.12) per kilo, almost half of the regular price, to a *revendedor* who was going to salt it and transport it further into the interior. The fisherman accommodated the hawker by accepting Cr$190 ($.11) per kilo as the wholesale price.

Hawkers who retire, leaving their suppliers during the winter months, usually resume other occupations. One man harvests coconuts in addition to selling fish. Another sells bread in Coqueiral and negotiates with suppliers during the summer only. A third went out of business in the winter because of an excess of debts and spent the time working in the small store he runs with his wife. He indicated, however, that he intended to start selling fish again in the summer, and several of the fishermen said that they would sell to him again. There was no question of his honesty, but merely a belief that he overextended himself during a difficult time of year. In actuality, his debts were incurred through speculation with large quantities of fish. He had established a salting station with a paid employee, but he went bankrupt when he was unable to sell the fish. He was forced to sell two rafts and an animal, and at least temporarily he lost all of his clients.

The fact that fish caught in abundance in the beach seines often are given away is a further indication of the limited market. For this same reason, several fish hawkers do the buying from each of the net owners in the summer, as no single vendor can handle the trade nor sustain the possible loss. It is the fish hawker who suffers most in an easily glutted market from a large increase in the catch, since he is required by convention to buy the fisherman's catch. This factor of high risk explains why the landholding owners of the beach seines do not become middlemen themselves. The "male nurse" of the Colônia de Pescadores' medical post decided to speculate with fish on one occasion. He returned from a trip to the Jitaí Lagoon with some 25 kilos of fish, but was unable to sell them because the catch from Coqueiral had already reached Guaiamu. He finally gave the fish to his brothers.

The large number of middlemen operates as a protective mechanism against the diminishing margins of profit by reducing the danger of excess loss to a few hawkers. It also explains why effective entrepreneurs have not risen from the ranks of the middlemen. Attempts at speculating with fish have largely met with failure. In 1955, a man from the state capital organized the fishermen into a single selling cooperative. He appealed to them through the promise of higher earnings and played on their long-standing opposition to the Colônia de Pescadores and the mayor's office. He promised that eventually they would receive better equipment in order to increase production. The undertaking failed because there was no adequate way to control the supply of fish to the consumer. Had the cooperative been able to furnish ice, although to do so was uneconomical in terms of the low volume of fish it was handling, it might have been able to store the fish, keep demand high, and maintain prices at least at the established ceiling. Eventually, a powerful cooperative might even have broken through the price controls. Without the means for preservation that would keep the fish in satisfactory condition for sale, however, prices fell sharply, and financial problems soon ended the cooperative.

[V I I]

Patterns of Ownership

JANGADEIROS in Coqueiral express a preference for independent production on their own log rafts during at least part of the year, particularly in the summer, when certain second-class species of fish migrate close to shore and weather conditions permit small rafts to go to sea. In the winter season heavy winds and seas often force the owner of a *bote* to sail on a larger and more sturdy craft, and during the Lenten season the demands for first-class species of fish encourage fishermen to enroll as crew members on someone else's raft. It was the same rationale which led to experimentation with and the rejection of hull sailboats in Coqueiral.

The seasonal variations in the fishing pattern account for some of the difficulties in making an accurate count of rafts in use in Coqueiral at any given time. In addition, the perishability of the jangada results in a constant change in the number of rafts on the beach. Old rafts always are being beached and new ones launched. Sometimes a fisherman uses both an old and new raft concurrently for a few weeks before the older one is retired from fishing. In an attempt to allow for such variation, a count of fishing equipment was taken on three separate occasions during the year, each in a different fishing season. To be certain that all rafts were present on the beach, the counts were made on holidays when no fishing was done.[1] A census of the fishing rafts in use was taken in April, October, and July, as part of a general household census and survey. Figures were then checked on the beach for accuracy. For the rafts used for coastal fishing see Table 12.

The number of rafts varies directly with the fishing season, as does the predominance of one type of raft over another. Thus, the number of *jangadas de alto* in use during the Lenten period increases, and a shift to *botes,* both of the *de remo* and *à vela* types, is evident in the

93

TABLE 12. NUMBER OF RAFTS ACCORDING TO FISHING SEASON

RAFT TYPE	LENT	WINTER	SUMMER
Jangada de alto	37	32	17
Paquete	31	29	44
Botes	25	30	37[a]

[a] 28 *botes de remo* and 9 *botes à vela*.

summer months. The number of *paquetes* also increases significantly in the summer months, since they can be used for both fishing strategies. The over-all count of rafts diminishes somewhat in the winter.

It is important to note that not all of the rafts on the beach at Coqueiral are used every day. Weather conditions often prevent rafts from sailing. Furthermore, if a raft is at sea for a number of hours, it must be beached for a time so that it can dry out. Even when it is used on alternate days, a *jangada de alto* lasts only slightly more than a year, after which time the logs must be replaced. Substitutions must be made for some logs before others, since lighter and drier wood becomes waterlogged more readily. A *paquete* lasts somewhat longer than a *jangada de alto*—that is, for about one and one-half years—and requires less time for drying on the beach. A *bote* can fish every day and still last up to two years or more since it spends much less time per day in the water. A *bote* can also be propped on its side so that the logs will dry thoroughly in the hot sun.

Frequently, the accoutrements of an old raft are used on a new one, and the logs are cut shorter and used temporarily for inshore fishing before they are completely discarded. Even then, there is always some apprentice fisherman or old man who will take advantage of the abandoned logs, no matter how waterlogged, to make a *bote de remo* for fishing near shore. Almost every mother in Coqueiral has a story of her son being carried off by the currents on a rebuilt raft. In one instance, fishermen rescued a young boy who had set out to fish on an abandoned raft rigged with a homemade sail. Upon reaching shore they called for help to push both their own and the rescued raft up on the beach. "Leave it there and get me an axe," the boy's mother responded. "That's one raft that won't sail again."

The cost of rafts is difficult to assess. Fishermen calculate the price of

Carpenter joining the logs of a new jangada

Complete tool kit for jangada construction

a jangada in terms of the cost of the logs delivered to Coqueiral, not according to the cost of construction. Since the size of the logs varies, there is no set price for them. Furthermore, many of the accoutrements of a raft often are salvaged from a previous craft, and no prices are

TABLE 13. PRICES OF JANGADA PARTS AND ACCOUTREMENTS IN COQUEIRAL

MATERIAL	JANGADA DE ALTO 8 x 1.5 m.	PAQUETE 7 x 1 m.	BOTE[a] 5 x 1 m.
Logs	Cr$75,000	Cr$28,000	Cr$11,000
Oar for rudder	4,000	2,000	2,000
Rowing oar	1,000	500	. .
Keelson	2,000	500	500
Centerboard	3,000	1,500	1,000
Captain's bench	200	200	200
Salting platform	500	200	. .
Uprights	500	200	200
Mast	1,000	500	250
Mast support	1,000	200	200
Boom	1,000	500	200
Sail	12,500	6,100	4,000
Anchor	300	200	200
Rope	7,000 (450 m.)	3,000 (180 m.)	2,000 (120 m.)
Basket for fish	1,000	300	300
Basket for bait	200	200	200
Wooden spoon for sail	300	300	300
Harpoon	1,000	600	. .
Kerosene lamp	750	750	. .
Straw mat	700	600	. .
Salt barrel	300	. .	. .
Knife	1,500	1,000	1,000
Gourds	500	500	200
Tree	200	200	100
Cooking pot	1,000	300	. .
Spoon for food	200	300	. .
Grapnel	500	500	. . .
Total	Cr$127,150 ($70)	Cr$48,250 ($27)	Cr$23,850 ($13)

[a] The price of a *bote de remo* can be calculated merely by deducting the mast, mast support, boom, and sail, reducing the price by Cr$4,650 ($2.50).

quoted for them. Although it takes a skilled carpenter several days to make a jangada, he charges only the Cr$1,000 ($.55) per day rate set for common day labor. The four men in Coqueiral who specialize in making jangadas all have other incomes, either from regular fishing or from pensions. They are each helped in the work of making a raft by the owner and several of his kinsmen, who charge nothing for their labor.

The cost of rafts, therefore, can be calculated only within a given range, and even then the differences in price categories blur between the smaller *jangadas de alto* and the larger *paquetes,* and between the smaller *paquetes* and the *botes à vela.* The prices quoted above were taken on the basis of three totally new, fully outfitted rafts and do not represent the actual annual or biannual expenditure for the replacement of equipment (see Table 13). The prices quoted for accoutrements refer to the cost of the wood exclusive of the labor involved in making the parts. This labor is included in carpenter's fees.

The price of hooks and line must be added in with the capital invested in the rafts themselves (see Table 14). The size of the hooks and the length and weight of the line used depend largely on the species of fish sought. The *jangada de alto* requires larger and more costly equipment, including longer and heavier line and rope, and a larger and more varied assortment of hooks. Generally speaking, anyone who can afford to build a raft can also manage to buy hooks and line. Such rudimentary gear is relatively inexpensive, and, although the owner of a raft supplies the equipment as well as the food for his crew, no fisherman finds himself compelled to fish on someone else's raft for want of fishing tackle.

Despite the greater over-all expenditure required to become the owner of a *jangada de alto,* local bigwigs prefer to buy the larger rafts because of their greater earning potential and the higher-quality species of fish accessible to them. As previously mentioned, the cost of a *jangada de alto* is higher, and the owner is required to supply both bait and food to the crew. He must pay 10% of his share of the catch plus a portion of fish for home consumption to a bait supplier when he is unable or unwilling to obtain bait for himself. By way of compensation, however, the possibility of catching fish is increased in proportion to the number of fishermen in a crew, and the over-all catch per day tends

TABLE 14. PRICES OF HOOKS AND LINE IN COQUEIRAL

EQUIPMENT	COSTS		
	Jangada	Paquete	Bote
Line	Cr$19,300	Cr$10,000	Cr$5,000
	(900 m.)	(400 m.)	(200 m.)
Wire	1,000	500	300
	(10 m.)	(5 m.)	(4 m.)
Nylon	1,600	350	210
	(20 m.)	(10 m.)	(6 m.)
Plumb	1,500	1,000	. .
Lead weights	2,500	1,000	250
Hooks	4,000	1,500	500
Total	Cr$29,900	Cr$14,350	Cr$6,260
	($17)	($8)	($4.50)

to be larger. Then, too, the average weight per catch is greater, since fish caught in the deeper waters plied by a *jangada de alto* are generally larger.

The cost of food is always deducted prior to the regular division of the catch. In exchange for a fisherman's labor, food is a negligible investment on the part of a jangada owner. The diet on a raft consists largely of *farinha,* or manioc flour, and fried fish. A gourd is filled with drinking water. Coconut husks are used for cooking fuel in an improvised stove placed on the wetted-down salting platform. A jangada carrying two or three men requires more food than a *paquete* because of the additional hours it spends at sea. A *bote,* which usually returns to shore after only a few hours, carries only a small *merenda,* or snack, consisting of a piece of fried fish and a few mouthfuls of manioc flour. The daily expenditure for food and fuel for a crew out fishing is listed in Table 15.

TABLE 15. EXPENDITURES FOR FOOD AND FUEL
(per day of fishing)

ITEM	JANGADA DE ALTO	PAQUETE
Manioc flour	Cr$800 (10 liters)	Cr$400 (5 liters)
Fried fish	(½ kilo)	(½ kilo)
Matches	60 (3 boxes)	60 (3 boxes)
Total	Cr$860 ($.47)	Cr$460 ($.25)

The owner of a *jangada de alto* also enjoys potentially higher earnings by an arrangement with his crew, who must give him a large share of their catch. While this is certainly a satisfactory arrangement, and may even be essential from the point of view of the entrepreneur, peasant fishermen are financially better off fishing on their own small rafts for at least part of the year. In effect, jangadeiros would rather be the owner of a *bote* than either the captain or a crew member on a jangada during the summer. The owner of a *bote* actually takes home more food for his family (see Table 16), and the low cost of a small raft and its minimal equipment make it readily replaceable year after year. Furthermore, the independent producer keeps all the fish he catches.

TABLE 16. FISH TAKEN FOR HOME CONSUMPTION
(per fisherman)

TYPE OF RAFT	FISH CONSUMED IN ONE MONTH (in kilos)	
	winter	*summer*
Jangada de alto	17.6	18.6
Paquete	17.5	20.5
Bote à vela	20	37
Bote de remo	23	25

Examination of the differential earnings of owners and crew of the four rafts in our sample explains the fishermen's preference for independent production on small rafts in the summer (see Table 17). Even the incredibly low summer earnings of $6 per month for the owner of a *bote de remo* were higher than the $5 per month earned by members of the crew of a large jangada. The earnings of the owner-operator of the *bote à vela* were higher because the sail-driven raft was able to stay out longer hours and go to greater distances than its oar-propelled counterpart. In the case of the *jangada de alto*, the owner did not fish on board, but was instead a retired fisherman who entrusted the raft to a nephew and a crew member of his choice in exchange for half of the catch. His best month provided the owner with only $14.50; however, the earnings of each member of the crew were reduced to just

$5. The earnings of the owner of the *paquete* ($16.30 in the winter season) were the highest, as he fished with his son, and their cash incomes were combined. The share system prevailed, since each sold his fish separately to one of the father's two sisters. However, the son's earnings reverted to his household, giving it the largest single income of any of the four rafts.

TABLE 17. DIFFERENTIAL EARNINGS OF OWNERS AND CREW
FOR SAMPLE ONE-MONTH PERIOD

TYPE OF RAFT	WINTER (July-Aug.)		SUMMER (Sept.-Oct.)	
	owner	crew	owner	crew
Jangada de alto	Cr$26,500 ($14.50)	Cr$13,250 ea. ($7)	Cr$17,450 ($9.60)	Cr$8,725 ea. ($5)
Paquete	30,300 ($16.30)	7,575 ea. ($4.20)	25,900 ($13,80)	6,475 ea. ($3.50)
Bote à vela	14,100 ($7.80)		21,000 ($12)	
Bote de remo	8,700 ($5)		10,800 ($6)	

In the share system a crew member must expend twice the time and energy that he would need to earn the same amount as an independent producer. As Table 9 indicates, on larger rafts both the sailing time and fishing time are significantly increased in the quest for first-class species of fish. Price controls which scarcely distinguish between the different classes of fish offer little incentive for a fisherman to stay out longer hours and share half of his catch, especially when the fish may not even be marketable in the summer months. Furthermore, owing to their abundance, the majority of fish caught on a large raft are of second-class variety, regardless of the season, so that a lone fisherman can catch more fishing within the reef on his own *bote* when the summer calm prevails.

The owner of a *jangada de alto* hesitates to use his raft near to shore for catching second-class species of fish, since the smaller weights of these catches do not afford him large earnings, even with the share system. It is considered more practical to alternate a costlier raft with a smaller one than to risk shortening the life span of the larger raft, which can be used more effectively further out to sea.

Of the sixty-nine individual raft owners in Coqueiral in July, 1965, seventeen had two rafts each, and three owned three rafts each. These were all combinations of large and small rafts, which never fished simultaneously, but were used to spell each other on alternate days or in different seasons, according to the prevailing fishing pattern. Most owner-operators of large rafts also prefer to have a small raft so that they can fish alone on days when they are unable to assemble a crew. Thus, the majority of those who own and operate two rafts use them to their own personal advantage rather than for specifically entrepreneurial activity. Only five of the owners of two or more rafts do not fish themselves. Nonfishing owners, for the most part, are unable to maintain a steady crew over the summer months and must withdraw from summer fishing activities.

A grave injustice would be done to jangadeiros if their preference for independent production were attributed merely to a distaste for sharing. Broadly speaking, a great deal of cooperation is evident among the jangadeiros of Coqueiral. A certain amount of social antagonism does pervade the daily life of the village, particularly in the relationships between fishermen and the local bigwigs. There is often some strife among fishermen and their families as well. However, the villagers of Coqueiral share a preoccupation with life and with their mutual problems, and they are always willing to extend a helping hand. An obvious example is the concern shown by the villagers as a whole that each participant on the beach seines receive his rightful share of the catch. In one case, a retired fisherman left the beach in disgust when he saw that there would not be enough fish to divide among the shore crew. The others demanded that a portion of fish be taken from the owner's share and delivered to the old man's house.

This spirit of cooperation also manifests itself in the act of raft fishing. It has already been noted that a variety of signals are used to announce that bait is available from a *lambuda* net, that fish are biting, or that danger is at hand. In addition, two sets of tools for making rafts and three spindles for twining cord are always loaned without charge although they belong to private owners. Even rafts and fishing tackle are loaned out: the owner receives a percentage of the catch, but irregular earnings of this kind hardly compensate him for the risk of possible damage to the equipment.

While there is a distinct occupational grouping of crew members in Coqueiral, it is at best a temporary category. Only twenty-three fishermen in Coqueiral are permanent members of jangada crews. Nine of these are single men under twenty-five years of age, who have not as yet obtained their own rafts. One or two are old men who have given up the cares of ownership because they no longer have the eyesight necessary to mark the fishing spots nor the vitality to sail to them. Three others are married men between twenty-five and twenty-nine years of age whose family responsibilities have not allowed them the extra capital needed to invest in a raft. Only the remaining eight can be classed among the minority in the village who prefer to spend their income on *cachaça* or marijuana, thereby diminishing their capacity for independent production.

It should be emphasized that not all jangadas go out fishing on the same day. Since the rafts must spend alternate days drying on the beach, it is rare to see more than thirty rafts sailing out of the bay. Again, perhaps only half of this number fish with more than one man, so that there are always idle fishermen available to form a crew. In addition, twelve owners of *botes* serve as regular crewmen on *jangadas de alto* owned by someone else. Others switch back and forth between their own rafts and any other they encounter on a given day. The owner or captain of a beached jangada always is willing to take a crewman's place on a raft. Crewing proves advantageous for all concerned, since the additional fish caught add to the owner's earnings and the fisherman is spared an idle day on the beach.

Since a fisherman can benefit most by alternating between independent production and acting as a crew member, a regular accommodation on a larger raft would appear to be important. There is some regularity in crew composition, especially between kinsmen. Four of the larger *jangadas de alto* fish with three men, including the owner and a two-man crew comprised of at least one kinsman. One raft engages two cousins, another, a brother and his cousin, and a third, a brother and his brother-in-law. In one case, an owner and his son sail with a nonkin member of the crew, who fishes "separate line" and divides his catch with them. In none of these cases does the income from the catch remain in one household. Rather, the customary share system is followed and it seems that the financial arrangements are not conditioned by kinship. The crews are organized as a mutually beneficial arrangement for both owner and fisherman. Of the twenty who are captains of other people's rafts, only two have kinsmen on their crews.

Thirteen of the twenty-five rafts on which the owner himself fishes fail to maintain steady crews. These owners gather varied personnel encountered on the beach at the time of sailing. Nine other owner-operators fish with kinsmen, among them a son, a brother, a nephew, two cousins, and four brothers-in-law. In three other cases, owner-operators fish with *compadres*, or fictive kin, but their relationship was not a prerequisite to their fishing partnerships.

Not all of the twenty nonfishing owners in Coqueiral purchased their rafts for entrepreneurial activities. Eight are retired fishermen who use their pensions to buy rafts for younger kinsmen, and in return they receive some proportion of the catch. In three other cases, non-fishing owners have kinsmen as captains, but the division of the catch is on a regular share basis. The share system is also followed in the nine remaining cases, in which nonrelated captains fish on rafts belonging to agriculturalists and fish hawkers who seek a profit.

The flexibility in crew composition enables fishermen to conduct relatively independent economic activities to their best personal advantage. The facility with which rafts were once obtained, however, is fast coming to an end, as wood resources diminish and logs become increasingly more costly. The source of supply of jangada wood in the state of Alagoas is receding constantly into the interior, and the size of the logs grows ever smaller. Indeed, a study recently undertaken at the University of California at Berkeley indicates that the quantity of wood formerly abundant in one county is now insignificant.[2]

The slow disappearance of the wood resources over the years has, without doubt, brought about certain changes in the pattern of fishing. The increasing cost of larger logs encourages the use of *paquetes* and *botes,* and the total number of man-hours spent fishing for first-class species of necessity diminishes. Older fishermen bemoan the fact that larger rafts used to be more common and that fishing at the edge of the continental shelf is becoming less frequent. The decision not to fish in the outer grounds obviously is influenced by the negligible difference in the margin of profit between first-class and second-class species of fish, but the general decrease in the size of available logs and the subsequent increase in the cost of larger logs, and hence of rafts, is also a contributing factor.

In order to purchase a large raft it now is necessary to depend on outside income. Some thirty years ago, jangadeiros were able to buy larger rafts while they were young and still single. Young men of today find it more difficult. Thus, out of approximately seventy respondents, those between ten and twenty-five years of age seem to have had difficulty in obtaining even a small raft with their earnings from fishing. Eleven of the twenty-three unmarried fishermen in Coqueiral are owners of rafts, but four in the ten- to nineteen-year-old group received their *botes* and *paquetes* as gifts from older kinsmen. One young man in the twenty- to twenty-four-year-old group bought a used raft. In all, eleven of the *botes* (more than one-third) and three of the *paquetes* (approximately one-tenth) in use in July were bought used. All of the rafts owned by these young men were of the smaller sizes.

The majority of owner-operators of rafts in Coqueiral are over twenty years of age and married. All but one of the owners of two or more rafts are married. The bulk of the nonfishing owners of *jangadas de alto* are agriculturalists between the ages of forty and fifty-five who have incomes from other sources to invest in fishing. Four of them also own one or another of the large nets in the village.

Most young men can now accumulate enough cash for the purchase of a raft only if they fish outside the village for a time, or if they have help from their families. In 1965 six young men went to Aracajú, where they fish for first-class species of fish on hull sailboats. There they earn Cr$900 ($.50) per kilo, more than twice the ceiling price in Coqueiral, and they are able to accumulate some capital in spite of the share system. In the winter, however, the entrance to the harbor in Aracajú becomes extremely dangerous and the fishermen are forced to return to Coqueiral, where they fish with someone else or use their earnings to buy their own rafts. Still, the majority of fishermen prefer to wait out the entire year in Coqueiral. They depend on the combined incomes of their families and a place on someone's jangada to get them through the winter. Then, in the summer, they use their own rafts for independent production.

[VIII]

Credit, Capital, and Savings

THE CONTINUED low earnings of raft fishermen—far below the Cr$36,900 ($20) monthly minimum wage established for the region— make necessary the full participation of all members of the extended family in the economic life of the village. The majority of the households in Coqueiral comprise a man, his wife, and their children. Yet, the functioning economic unit often includes several such nuclear families. If it were not for the cooperation of all members of an extended family and the neighbors who sometimes assume the obligations of kinsmen, it would be impossible to maintain a minimum livelihood. The family acts, therefore, as a single productive and banking unit that goes through some of the complex economic motions usually associated with more developed economies.

Despite the obvious poverty, a visitor to Coqueiral is quick to notice groups of fishermen engaged in idle conversation on the beach or sleeping in the shade of the coconut palms. This idleness is temporary and reflects neither laziness nor irresponsibility. Rather, it is the fact that a raft must dry on the beach after a day at sea that keeps a group of fishermen on shore. Others are resting on the beach after spending a hazardous night on an ocean-bound raft. Some are unable to fish because of the chronic shortage of bait. Much of their time is spent tending to the rafts, helping to mend a net, or engaging in a variety of tasks connected both with fishing and with the daily round of living.

A fisherman's failure to seek out additional work reflects only the lack of opportunity for employment in Coqueiral. At the time of my study only fifteen fishermen supported themselves with secondary occupations, ranging from barber to day laborer. These offered only a small supplement to the monthly earnings from fishing. When some opportunity for wage work does appear, however, there are many fishermen who take advantage of it. Thus, several hundred days of wage work at Cr$1,ooo ($.55) per day were used up in less than two weeks' time by fishermen working on the construction of a government-sponsored breeding tank for bait. Fishermen also complained that jobs in connection with the construction of the market that houses the weigh-in scale went to workers from Guaiamu rather than to the villagers.

The limited opportunity for adding to individual earnings encourages the formation of an extended economic unit. The obligations among kinsmen to supplement each other's earnings are not stated in strict rules, nor is it always easy to assess exactly in which direction a person's obligations lie. Rather, the sense of obligation follows from a feeling of responsibility on the part of individuals to combine their earning power. This sense of responsibility is more highly developed between the generations than it is among siblings.

Despite a certain amount of rivalry among siblings, a high degree of cooperation can be expected. In most cases, quarreling erupts because of excessive drinking, which often affects the family income. In other cases, alleged laziness on the part of one adult member of a family frequently results in intrafamilial squabbling. In one particular case, a retired fisherman named Mestre Geraldo offered a raft to his son and son-in-law in the hope that they would fish together. The son-in-law refused, complaining that he would do all the work and that the son would contribute nothing to the arrangement. After considerable discussion, Mestre Geraldo finally gave the raft to his son-in-law, in the belief that his son would fend for himself with greater ease than his daughter, who was already overburdened with seven young children.

Even under extreme tensions, however, the family continues to function as a single economic unit. Mestre Geraldo's Cr$26,ooo ($14) monthly pension acts as the stabilizing base. Although they are grouped under three separate roofs, the families take many of their meals together, and there is constant sharing of food. A part of their cash income is also shared. Mestre Geraldo's wife, daughter, and daughter-in-law work together in the manufacture of straw baskets. In the month of July their combined income from the handicraft was approximately Cr$16,ooo ($8.8o). The children of working age help to gather straw, fish for bait, or collect mollusks. Mestre Geraldo's son-in-law earned approximately Cr$20,ooo ($11) on the *bote à vela* in July. His son com-

bined gill net fishing with a few days of wage labor, earning approximately Cr$18,000 ($10) during the same month. The total earnings
for the entire family in the month of July came to approximately
Cr$80,000 ($44), just slightly above the monthly salary paid to each of
the staff members of the defunct medical post.

FIGURE 3. SAMPLE EXTENDED-FAMILY NETWORK

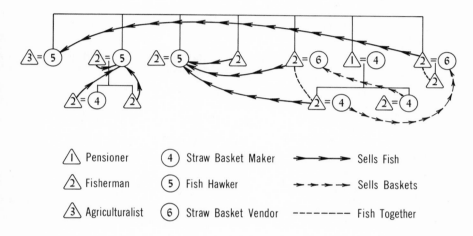

⚊⚊⚊➤	Sells Fish				

Pensioner   Straw Basket Maker   Sells Fish

Fisherman   Fish Hawker   Sells Baskets

Agriculturalist   Straw Basket Vendor   Fish Together

The extended-family unit does not really end here, but ramifies
throughout the village (see Figure 3). Mestre Geraldo's siblings may
be taken as an example of the spreading network of economic relationships. His three brothers are all fishermen, two of whom are married to
straw basket vendors. One of these brothers fishes on a *paquete* with
his son. Another fishes together with Mestre Geraldo's son, using
rented gill nets. A third, unmarried, brother fishes alone on his own
small raft. All three of Mestre Geraldo's sisters are fish hawkers, two of
whom are married to fishermen. The eldest buys fish from her unmarried brother and from her brother and nephew who fish with the gill
nets. The middle sister buys from her own two sons, her husband, and
her nephew who fishes on the *paquete*. The nephew's father sells to the
youngest sister.

In some cases it is difficult to determine exactly where a household begins and ends. Although customarily a new couple takes up residence in a separate house, the couple usually retains close ties with the parental households and often lives next door. Members of one household can be found in one of the others' during the day, and the sharing of food and labor is common.

Sometimes the lines of authority in these multi-household units are obscure. Authority does not always rest with the principal wage earner, but is usually vested in the eldest male, even though he may be incapacitated and dependent upon his children or grandchildren for support. Alternately, an elderly woman may be the titular head of an extended family and contribute substantially to family income. Yet, she will have little to say with regard to investment decisions.

Children of working age are an obvious economic boon, and several households in Coqueiral undertake the rearing other people's children, many of them nonkin. The extent of such behavior is difficult to determine, since a child may continue to sleep in his own household while taking meals with a neighbor. In such cases, the neighbor's advice is always sought with regard to decisions affecting the child. When a kinsman is involved, he may even exercise ultimate authority over the child. Although children, especially girls, contribute significantly to household income, there are several cases in which a family is feeding a nonresident young fisherman, despite the fact that his earnings revert to his own household and not to theirs. There are also innumerable examples of foster children who are not yet of working age. There is some expectation of eventual reciprocity involved in such acts of giving, but, for the most part, the convention springs from mutual pity and neighborly good will.

Without question, the diet in Coqueiral is deficient. Small children are fed on gruel rather than fish, and they manifest many symptoms of protein malnutrition.[1] Adults often complain of waiting far into the night for the day's only meal. A certain amount of protein is obtained through raft fishing, but a jangadeiro's family must supplement its regular diet by subsistence fishing from the reef and collecting mollusks in the mangrove swamp. The combined 57 kilos of fish taken home in July by Mestre Geraldo's son-in-law and son were meant to supply the animal protein requirements of eight adults and nine children for one month. In addition, Mestre Geraldo earned a small share of fish on the few occasions that he helped pull a beach seine to shore. Fruits in season, coconuts, and the greens from a small garden plot that Mestre Geraldo blocked out on an island in the mangrove swamp, afford the only home-grown supplements to the diet. Still, additional food staples must be purchased to meet the normal caloric requirements. Meat is rarely consumed in Coqueiral, but salt, coffee, sugar, manioc flour, and some beans usually are bought. All other foods are luxury items consumed only by the commercial coconut planters. Clothing and medicines add to the weekly drain on income that flows to the county capital. On one occasion, a single medical prescription cost Mestre Geraldo Cr$13,000 ($7.20), or half of his monthly retirement pay.

TABLE 18. EARNINGS AND DEBTS OF PENSIONER'S FAMILY
(July, 1965)

	EARNINGS	DEBTS
Women	Cr$16,000	. .
Mestre Geraldo	26,000	Cr$2,000
Son-in-law	20,000	15,250
Son	18,000	24,700
Total	Cr$80,000 ($44)	Cr$39,950 ($22)

With the constant drain on money through taxes and living expenses, it is not surprising that almost every family in Coqueiral finds itself several thousand *cruzeiros* in debt at all times. Table 18 compares the monthly income of Mestre Geraldo's family to their standing debts in July, 1965. His son-in-law owed a total of Cr$3,250 ($1.10) to three local storekeepers. His own debt to the Colônia de Pescadores amounted to over Cr$12,000 ($6.60) for some 40 kilos of fish. Mestre Geraldo's son had borrowed Cr$8,000 ($4.40) from the Benevolent Society to pay a long-standing debt in the stores. In addition, he owed Cr$1,700 ($.94) to the fishermen's guild and another Cr$15,000 ($8.30) to relatives in Rio de Janeiro. They had sent him the money the year before so that he could migrate to Rio, where they had a job waiting for him. However, the pressing needs of his family forced him to spend a part of that money in the village. While waiting to earn the difference for the bus ticket, he spent the rest and now talks distantly of his opportunity of going to Rio. Mestre Geraldo has managed to live on the income from his retirement pay, but still owes several *contos* (Cr$1,000) in local stores.

Food is bought in the seven local stores on credit, while basic cash purchases are made at the Saturday market, where a few *cruzeiros* can be saved on almost all items. Still, it costs more to make up the dietary deficiency in protein by buying beans (Cr$350, or $.18 per kilo) than a fisherman can earn selling second-class species of fish (Cr$300, or $.16 per kilo).[2] Thus fishermen prefer to sell first-class species of fish (Cr$400 or $.22 per kilo). They justify its sale by invoking the popular belief that "more fleshy fish cause stomach aches," as they are truly unaware of the fact that first-class fish have a higher protein yield. Unfortunately, since price controls on fish have not kept pace with the rapid inflation, even the sale of first-class species does not help the fishermen's "balance of payments."

In addition, a few cooking utensils and kerosene lamps along with fuel to light them must be bought either in the market or at local stores. When coconut husks are not available, cooking fuel is collected in the mangrove swamp, and only the local bigwigs purchase charcoal. A house costs little to construct, and often is built by a *mutirão*, a co-operative work party comprised of kinsmen and neighbors who eat, drink, and chant while completing the work. The wattle-and-daub houses of most of the jangadeiros are sparsely furnished, generally having little more than a bed, a table, and a couple of stools. Many of the fishermen, and especially the children, sleep on straw mats on the pounded mud floors. Meals are usually taken seated on the floor. Some items of clothing are bought, but most are made at home from store-bought cloth. Shoes are seldom worn, and only a few young men and children have them for dressy occasions. Even this small amount of clothing usually is bought on credit. When Sr. Nilo's sister, the school teacher, required that school children dress in uniforms for the Saint's Day celebrations, most of the villagers were forced to extend their credit in the local stores in order to purchase cloth.

This account is not intended to give the impression that wants are limited. Indeed, wants are infinitely expandable, as the patterns of consumption of the local bigwigs show. Moreover, the patterns of consumption for the jangadeiros themselves are expanding, since all villagers tend to emulate the city folk. The Guaiamu market is now flooded with ready-made clothes and with trinkets and plastic toys that flow up from the industrial south and are added to the villagers' list of wants. These items are quickly replacing the string and shell amulets worn by the majority of the villagers, and the wooden trucks and coconut husk toys enjoyed by the children. The new, manufactured items are paid for in cash, while credit is used in the local stores.

A system of credit and savings thereby is essential not only for subsistence in the lean winter months but also as a means of freeing capital for cash purchases. A system of credit exists in Coqueiral, but it cannot sustain cash loans in large amounts. Rather, the system allows for small running debts in one or two of the seven local stores for food and other household needs. A customer builds up a debt of approximately Cr$2,000 ($1.10) in one store and then must go to another. All accounting is done in duplicate notebooks, one kept by the storekeeper and the other by the customer. The possibility of a storekeeper making large cash loans for equipment is severely limited since the low buying power of the villagers restricts the amount of liquid capital at hand. This is reflected in the paucity of goods for sale in the local stores, even during the summer months when a tourist market for goods does exist. All of the stores carry food staples and a few dry goods, as well as the inexpensive sugar cane alcohol, *cachaça*. But beer, butter, dried meat, and other luxury items can be obtained only in the county seat.

Some liquid capital becomes available in the village through the sale of straw products, mainly of baskets. This handicraft industry provides the basis for a carefully balanced system of credit. The household survey and census shows that the straw industry accounts for a large part of the village income, especially during the winter months when fishing activities are slowed by weather conditions. Monthly income from basketry reaches nearly Cr$1,000,000 ($550) in the winter months. This income allows families to pay their debts in the local stores. Payment for baskets is made every fifteen days, when the local vendors return to the village from their selling trips abroad. At this time, each household pays at least part of its debt to the storekeepers, thereby re-establishing credit for the next fifteen-day period.

A few handbags sold in the village are of a woven straw variety, often using banana leaves, local seeds, lining, and shellac for a decorative effect. These sell to tourists for up to Cr$2,000 ($1.10) apiece in the summer. The majority of items are baskets, made in far less time in a basic grill-like pattern, sometimes with a few dyed pieces of straw woven into a simple design. These baskets wholesale for Cr$350 ($.18) apiece in the village.

Some 214 women are directly engaged in the manufacture of straw products. Nearly three thousand baskets were manufactured in the month of July. A few are sold to visitors in the village, but most are taken to the state capitals and interior markets extending from Recife to Salvador. Some of the better baskets are resold in bulk at Cr$450 ($.25) and find their way as far south as Rio de Janeiro. Every fifteen days seven women each take approximately two hundred bags to the interior markets where the bags retail for Cr$600 ($.33) apiece. Although the bags are not taxed at the interstate borders, the vendors must pay for their own transportation and additional living expenses. As in the case of the fish hawkers, they prefer to minimize their risk by selling out quickly in bulk for less profit and returning to the village sooner.

The importance of the straw industry is indicated by the fact that 81 out of the 102 households that receive their principal income from some aspect of the fishing industry also engage in the production or sale of straw products. Twenty-one out of 28 households whose principal income is derived from agriculture also produce or market straw items. Of the 30 households whose heads are involved in the coconut harvest, carpentry, and wage work, 27 take part in some aspect of the straw industry. Most of the 38 households without resident males also support themselves from the manufacture or sale of straw products.

Women of the poorest agricultural households may work in the straw industries since the cultivation of a field of one or two *tarefas* does not require their full participation, except perhaps at harvest time. In cases where larger agricultural plots are at stake, the women are precluded from taking an active part in straw manufacture because their presence is required in the fields. Women whose husbands have large coconut holdings do not work with straw, but limit their activities to work around the house. Their daughters often occupy themselves with less commercial tasks, such as sewing. The acquisition of a sewing

Woman weaving a straw basket. Her wares are displayed in the window.

machine and attendance at sewing classes costing Cr$1,000($.55) per month is a good indication of greater economic stability and of social mobility in Coqueiral. In general, with the attainment of some degree of economic stability, women tend to leave more entrepreneurial activities behind and engage in less commercial endeavors.

While women play an important role in the accumulation of capital, they do not participate directly in decisions regarding the investment of capital. Men playfully refer to the women as the *manda-chuvas* (rainmakers), or "the boss," in the winter months when their earnings from the straw industry may exceed those of their mates. Still, it is rare that a man will seek his wife's advice regarding the purchase of fishing equipment. In 1965 only one woman in Coqueiral owned a raft. It had belonged to her husband, who had abandoned her. She had no relatives in the village other than her children, and her eldest son was only eleven years old. She entrusted her raft to a young neighbor with whom she shared half of the catch, but she did not plan to replace the raft the following year. Another woman, also abandoned by her husband, cared for coconut palms that he had planted in the mangrove swamp. She also ventured into a high-interest-rate loan scheme, charging an elderly fisherman 50% on a cash loan that he used to pay his retirement fees. She was so much criticized by the community for her behavior that she declared that she never would loan money again. She also rejected an invitation to be a member of the Benevolent Society. In still a third case, a woman who was the innovator of the straw industry twenty-five years before, and whose income combined with that of her four daughters far exceeded her husband's, decided to buy a store. She intended to use the money that she had accumulated as cook for the owner of the sugar mill at his summer house. Her husband, who doubled as breadman and fish hawker, would not allow it and criticized her sharply for not having more investment sense.

It is important to note that in most cases the earnings from the straw industry do not go directly into the purchase of fishing equipment. On the whole, women's and men's earnings alike go directly into the household, where they are thrown into a common pot to meet the family's basic needs. A son's earnings are turned over immediately to the head of the household, who may or may not let him keep some for the purchase of cigarettes or *cachaça*. A household's production of straw baskets is sold as common stock, and the money earned enters into the household budget.

Even as the peasant fishing family struggles to acquire the bare necessities, the need to save up for the purchase of equipment confronts them. Where previously logs were given to fishermen by *patrões* in exchange for fish, diminishing forest resources have made logs a focus of speculation. The increased distance of the source of supply from the beach precludes the possibility of bartering with fresh fish, and plantation owners now prefer to sell logs to middlemen. Only nine of the rafts currently in use in Coqueiral were given as gifts to the fishermen by landholding *patrões*. The delivery of logs by middlemen to the beach at Coqueiral is convenient for the fishermen, who do not have to arrange for woodsmen to fell the trees nor for oxcarts to transport the logs to the village.

These new arrangements, however, require cash for all transactions. Few rafts, if any, are bought either on credit or with cash from a loan. The inability to accumulate cash income from fishing for reinvestment means that the replacement fund (Wolf 1966:5–6) must be supplemented from outside the fishing economy. Purchases of logs for rafts usually take place in the summer, when the increased yield from the sea, combined with the increased sales from straw products, afford the villagers the opportunity to accumulate necessary capital. Production in the straw bag industry increases in the summer with the greater facility for drying straw. Also, more women enter into the industry in the summer, when they are freed from the necessity of collecting in the mangrove swamp. Moreover, children are freed from their subsistence tasks and can help to gather straw.

Earnings are never so high as to mitigate the effects of the long winter season, however. Just as there are more fish hawkers in the summer fishing season, so the number of straw vendors also increases. In this way, the effects of increased production are not enjoyed by any one person, but again are distributed throughout the community. Furthermore, increments in summer wages and production are not sustained over a long enough period to enable a household to recover financially. Soon there is a reversion to the hardships of the winter and a reliance on the debt-credit system to merely stay alive. During the summer some savings can be accumulated to offset, however slightly, the poverty of winter.

In such a marginal economic situation the systematic storing up of even small sums of capital over long periods of time is impossible. Consumption needs far outweigh the desire to accumulate cash, and there is no notion of savings over and above normal household expenditures. Instead, at any given time money is diverted from the usual patterns of consumption in order to meet necessary expenses. Consequently, families tighten their belts and economize. Savings are accumulated, sometimes in the form of liquid cash, but more often in the form of hard goods, which are used for a time but can be sold at a later date. These are goods of high value, such as radios, which are considered an investment against possible future needs. Since the value of these goods has increased with the rising cost of such items in Brazil, they can always be sold at a profit, even long after the original purchase.

Another way of accumulating goods is to buy in bits and pieces against future use. Thus, various parts of a house, such as roof tiles or bricks, may be bought and stored over months, and even years, until enough exist to complete the construction. This is especially true in the purchase of a jangada. The logs are often left on the beach long after the necessary drying period because there is not enough money available to finish the essential accoutrements. In one case, a jangada was left for several months on the beach before work on it was completed, even though the logs had been given as a gift.

Perhaps the most important means of future savings in the village is through animal husbandry. Almost every household in Coqueiral owns some livestock or fowl as a form of savings. Sheep and goats feed on the tableland and pigs, in the mangrove swamp, resulting in a considerable reduction in the cost of their keep. Nevertheless, many villagers claim that the cost of feeding a pig is more than the animal is ultimately worth in cash value, unless it produces a number of offspring. The risk involved in animal husbandry is high; in certain years disease has decimated the entire livestock population. Still, livestock remains an important investment, since the sale of an animal supplies the cash necessary to conduct another transaction.

More than forty cash transactions involving livestock were reported for the three-month period from April to June, 1965. The total cash value of these transactions was reported as more than Cr$1,000,000 ($550). Twenty more transactions were said to have taken place the previous summer (October, 1964 to February, 1965) in the amount of more than Cr$500,000 ($275). It is likely that additional sales took place during this time and that many were forgotten or went unreported by informants. At least thirty of the reported sales of livestock directly coincided with the purchase of a raft, or specifically, of eleven *jangadas de alto*, eleven *paquetes*, and eight *botes*.

Given the limited possibilities of arranging for loans of cash in Coqueiral, the sale of animals, especially of pigs, becomes an essential source of liquid capital at the time of purchasing a raft. A large pig sells for up to Cr$60,000 ($33) and matures in about the same length of time required for the replacement of a raft, which is about one and one-half years. Since the logs must be dried for several months in the sun, the best time to replace a raft is in the summer. It is also in the summer that the combined incomes of the members of individual and multi-households yield sufficient cash to direct some of it toward reinvestment in equipment.

[IX]

Innovation and Change

WE HAVE examined the traditional economy in Coqueiral and the way in which it is maintained. It now remains to discuss the place of change in the peasant society. As previously stated, the prospects for change are affected seriously by the lines of stratification in the county as a whole. Local bigwigs have assumed positions of power that were made available as a result of the emigration of local elites and the general indifference of traditional elites still resident in the valley of Guaiamu. Formerly these elites had shown interest in the jangadeiros so long as they were supplied with an adequate amount of better-quality species of fish at low prices. In their traditional role of *patrão*, they often gave logs to the fishermen in exchange for fish. With the increase in the distance between the source of the logs and the beach, however, the supplying of fresh fish to the plantations became impossible. Planters now sell jangada wood to middlemen, and they leave the local bigwigs to regulate the economic affairs of the jangadeiros. As we have seen in Chapter III, the behavior of the local bigwigs has rather ominous consequences in terms of the possibilities for innovation and change.

Change in Coqueiral begins with these bigwigs and then spreads downward. This is because their position in the community gives them access to resources which the peasant fishermen do not have. Outright loans for equipment are not forthcoming, except in the rare case of a fisherman who still receives help from a *patrão*. Money for investment in innovations in the fishing economy comes from outside sources of wealth, such as coconut planting. Bigwigs are anxious to realize a return on their investment. Since the production on jangadas is very low, few local bigwigs own them as an entrepreneurial activity. They are likely to invest only in equipment which will give them a profit, and this does not always prove to be in the best interest of the fishermen.

Sr. Nilo, the president of the fishermen's guild, is often heard to remark that he "already experimented with everything." He has owned a corral, fish traps, shark hooks, a large drift net, and a hull sailboat, but he abandoned them all because, as he claims, "The fishermen were lazy and uncooperative!" All of the local bigwigs in Coqueiral cite instances in which they have introduced "more efficient fishing techniques" to the village, only to have them rejected. They, too, blame their failures at entrepreneurship on the "fishermen's lack of cooperation."

We have pointed out that the jangadeiro in Coqueiral is neither lazy nor uncooperative, but rather an industrious individual who would not arbitrarily reject an innovation unless it were in his own best interest to do so. The acceptance or rejection of innovations in Coqueiral can only be understood as a function of the social structure, which infringes on the lives of the local peasantry. In some instances, as in the case of nylon gill nets, fishermen willingly embraced change, even though the local bigwigs discouraged them. In other cases, such as the introduction of hull sailboats, technological innovation was rejected by jangadeiros even though it might have brought about a general increase in overall production. In both of these instances, jangadeiros were able to exercise their own will. Unfortunately, they cannot always do so.

Nylon gill nets are one example of an innovation that began with the local bigwigs. Sr. Mario, the secretary of the Benevolent Society, and his partner, the president, were the first people in Coqueiral to own a *caceia*. Their purchase was quickly followed by that of a group of fourteen local coconut planters and by the "male nurse," who hoped to catch first-class species of fish in the nets. The first fisherman to own gill nets bought two of them with a loan from a *patrão*. Another fisherman was given a net by a son who works in the state capital. When other fishermen showed interest in buying gill nets, however, they were discouraged by Sr. Nilo, who feared that the dogfish sharks caught with nets of this type soon would be the only fish on sale at the local market. Yet, the men who were fishing with *caceias* were earning far more from the sale of dogfish than the jangadeiros who were fishing with hooks and line. Nevertheless, without loans either from the fish-

N

SOUTH
AMERICA

AREA of DETAIL

FORTALEZA✱

MAJORLÂNDIA■

TIBAÚ■
CAIÇARA●

PITANGUÍ●
GENIPABÚ●
NATAL✱
BAÍA FORMOSA●

BAHIA de TRAIÇÃO●
CABADELLO●
JOÃO PESSOA✱
PENHA●
PITIMBÚ●
ACAÚ●
ITAPESSUMA■
RECIFE✱

SUAPE●
PORTO de GALINHAS●
TAMANDARÉ■

BARRA de SÃO ANTONIO●
MACEIÓ✱
FRANCES●
BARRA de SÃO MIGUEL●
COQUEIRAL●
PENEDO●

STUDY AREA

ARACAJÚ✱
MOSQUEIRO●

CONDE●
SITIO●

PRAIA de FORTE●
AREMBEPE●
SALVADOR✱

São Francisco
Guaiamu

Acarau

✱ STATE CAPITAL
■ COUNTY CAPITAL
● VILLAGES

KM   60   120

Map IV - NORTHEAST FISHING ZONE

TYPE OF CRAFT	TYPE OF EQUIPMENT	PRINCIPAL SPECIES OF FISH	MARKET	COMMENTS
LOG RAFTS PLANK RAFTS	LOBSTER TRAPS HANDLINES	LOBSTER, MACKEREL, PORGY, YELLOW TAIL, DOGFISH, SEA BASS	FORTALEZA	LOGS COME FROM STATE OF PARA IN AMAZON AND COST APPROX. Cr.$15,000 APIECE. LOBSTER FISHERMEN ARE PAID SALARIES BY COMPANIES WHO ALSO PAY THEIR DUES AND TAXES TO THE FISHERMEN'S GUILD. LOBSTER COMPANY IN MAJORLÂNDIA OWNS ALL OF THE RAFTS.
LOG RAFTS	LOBSTER TRAPS	LOBSTER		
HULL SAIL BOATS HULL SAIL BOATS PLANK RAFTS	HANDLINES, DIP NETS LOBSTER TRAPS BEACH SEINES	YELLOW FIN TUNA, HALFBEAK, FLYING FISH, YELLOWTAIL, MUTTONFISH, LOBSTER, SNAPPER	NATAL	LOBSTERS FISHED OUT AND COMPANIES WITH-DRAWING. LOG RAFTS WERE REPLACED BY PLANK RAFTS AND SAIL BOATS ABOUT FIFTY YEARS AGO. A HULL SAIL BOAT COSTS OVER A MILLION CRUZEIROS AND A PLANK RAFT COSTS APPROX. Cr.$700,000.
SAIL BOATS LOG RAFTS MOTOR BOATS	DIP NETS, DRAG NETS, HANDLINES	HALFBEAK, YELLOWFIN TUNA, MACKEREL, FLYING FISH, SARDINE, SHRIMP	LOCALLY JOÃO PESSOA	LOGS COST Cr.$20,000 EACH. SAIL BOATS COST ABOUT Cr.$600,000. MOTOR BOATS OWNED BY LOBSTER COMPANY. FISHERMEN PAID Cr.$100 PER KILO OF LOBSTER.
LOG RAFTS PLANK RAFTS PLANK CANOES	GILL NET, SHRIMP NET, DIP NET, HAND LINING. SEINES	MULLET, HALFBEAK, CATFISH, PORGY, SNAPPER	JOÃO PESSOA	LOGS COST Cr.$20,000 APIECE AND COME FROM STATE OF ALAGOAS. CANOES COST ABOUT Cr.$100,000 AND ARE FOUND AT RIVER MOUTHS AND ESTUARIES.
MIXED TECHNIQUES	VARIETY OF NETS, TRAPS, HANDLINES	MACKEREL, JACK, MUTTONFISH, SNAPPER, LOBSTER	RECIFE	MINGLING OF TECHNIQUES IN URBAN ZONES.
LOG RAFTS PLANK RAFTS SAIL BOATS MOTOR BOATS	HANDLINES, GILL NETS, LOBSTER TRAPS, SEINES	YELLOWTAIL, YELLOWFIN TUNA, TRIGGERFISH, DRUM, MUTTONFISH, DOGFISH, CARAPEBA, MULLET, LOBSTER, MACKEREL	RECIFE	MOTOR BOATS AND HULL SAIL BOATS OWNED BY LOBSTER COMPANIES. DIMINISHING RETURNS REPORTED IN LOBSTER FISHING
LOG RAFTS DUGOUT CANOES	HANDLINES, CASTNETS	MACKEREL, JACK, YELLOWTAIL, SNAPPER, SARDINE, MULLET, CATFISH.	LOCALLY, MACEIÓ	THE STATE OF ALAGOES IS THE MAJOR SOURCE OF LOGS FOR RAFTS IN BRAZIL
DUGOUTS	HANDLINES, CASTNETS	MULLET, SARDINE, CATFISH	LOCALLY	VILLAGE LOCATED ON LARGE ESTUARY.
LOG RAFTS	HANDLINES, GILLNETS, SEINES	CATFISH, BARBUDO, DOGFISH, MACKEREL, SNAPPER, DRUM, MULLET	LOCALLY	AREA OF EXTENSIVE ETHNOGRAPHIC RESEARCH REPORTED IN TEXT
PLANK CANOES	CASTNETS, CORRALS, HANDLINES, SEINES, LONGLINES	CATFISH, HAKE, RAY, CARAPEBA, SHRIMP, MULLET, SNOOK	ARACAJÚ	THIS AREA OF THE COAST IS GREATLY INFLUENCED BY THE WATERS OF THE SÃO FRANCISCO RIVER AND MANY SMALLER RIVERS IN THE STATE OF SERGIPE.
LOG RAFTS	HANDLINES, SEINES	SNAPPER, GROUPER, YELLOWTAIL, DOGFISH, MACKEREL	LOCALLY	OPEN BEACHES WITH STRONG SURF. LOGS FOR RAFTS COME FROM THE STATE OF BAHIA. SITIO HAS 25 RAFTS AND BAXIAS HAS FEWER THAN 20.
OPEN SAIL BOATS	HANDLINES	SNAPPER, YELLOWTAIL, HAKE, MACKEREL, JACK, MULLET	SALVADOR	FISHING IN ARAMBEPE STUDIES BY KOTTAK (1966)
MIXED TECHNIQUES	VARIETY OF NETS, TRAPS, HANDLINES	YELLOWTAIL, DOGFISH, MACKEREL, SNAPPER, JACK	SALVADOR	MINGLING OF TECHNIQUES IN URBAN ZONE.

----- STATE BOUNDARY
············· CONTINENTAL SHELF

ermen's guild, which were not forthcoming, or from the Benevolent Society, which charges prohibitive interest rates, there was little likelihood that other fishermen would be able to buy nets for themselves.

It is important to remember here that one of the principal interests of the local bigwigs is to maintain a supply of inexpensive first-quality species of fish to the Guaiamu market, in the hope of retaining the favor of the planters from whom they derive their power. The system of price controls applies only to first-class species of fish. Second-class and third-class species bring the same prices in Coqueiral as in other ports. However, first-class species of fish are sold at approximately half the price charged in other ports and for only Cr$100 ($.06) per kilo more than second-class species. This minimal price differential is one of the main reasons why jangadeiros prefer to sell their own catch of second-class species rather than share half of a catch of first-class fish with the owner of a boat.

It was an interest in supplying first-class species of fish to the Guaiamu market that brought about the introduction of hull sailboats to Coqueiral. Local bigwigs saw an opportunity to earn a relatively large profit on the sale of the better-quality fish. They were not interested in doing the fishing themselves, but wanted to invest their capital in the productive labors of fishermen. By grouping six or seven formerly independent producers on larger vessels, they were able to exploit a relatively inexpensive labor force by means of the share system.

Hull sailboats were not new to the jangadeiros. European-style sailboats were used to haul sugar and salt from Coqueiral, and an occasional fishing boat took safe harbor in the bay. Furthermore, many of the jangadeiros from Coqueiral had fished outside of the village in major ports and were familiar with commercial fishing vessels. The local bigwigs assumed that the fishermen would be eager to accept membership in a crew. They counted on the fact that jangadeiros were accustomed to the share system and that they would readily adapt themselves to it on a permanent basis.

The cooperative behavior that characterizes the productive phases of raft fishing is not manifest when a fisherman is working for an entrepreneur motivated by a desire for profit. Fishermen were willing to abide by the share system in the winter months on boats which afforded them considerably more comfort than the largest of jangadas.

However, in the summer, they wanted to fish on their own small log rafts. They were merely following their customary pattern of alternation between fishing as a member of a crew and fishing independently to their own personal advantage. After all, jangadeiros fishing on their own log rafts were able to earn as much as they could on a hull sailboat and in just half the time. Moreover, the Cr$100 ($.06) per kilo difference between first-class and second-class species of fish was not enough of an incentive for them to continue on hull sailboats in the summer months when fish were biting in abundance just offshore. Only in other ports without price controls were earnings significantly increased to a point where sharing of the catch was warranted.

The local bigwigs were not willing to raise the price on first-class species of fish in Coqueiral for fear of angering local planters, even though by doing so they also would have been increasing their own profit. At the same time, they were not willing to allow their boats to fish outside of Coqueiral's fishing grounds, where they would be unable to scrutinize the catch. They were prepared to earn less locally rather than risk being cheated by the fishermen. Whereas jangadeiros who own large rafts adapt themselves to the loss of a crew by fishing on their small rafts during the summer, the local bigwigs did not want to see their investment idle on the beach for that period of time. Unable to force jangadeiros to remain on the sailboats in the summer, they preferred to sell the boats rather than use them only part-time.

Sr. Nilo, the president of the Colônia de Pescadores, was the first person to introduce hull sailboats to Coqueiral in 1953. Using money which he earned from a number of non-fishing activities, Sr. Nilo purchased a boat which was approximately nine meters long and which had a covered deck divided into two compartments. Fish could be stored in the rear hatch, and fishermen could sleep or take refuge from the weather in the forward hatch. The boat sailed with seven fishermen who used hooks and line. Sr. Nilo supplied the fishing tackle, but he always took out his expenses before dividing the catch with the crew. The share system was the customary one of *meiacão*, half for Sr. Nilo and half to be divided among the members of the crew. The captain, Mestre Geraldo, earned an additional 5% of the catch from Sr. Nilo's share.

Before coming to fish on the sailboat, Mestre Geraldo had alternated between a large jangada owned by Sr. Nilo and his own small raft. In fact, Sr. Nilo claims to have built his fishing boat with Mestre Geraldo in mind. Mestre Geraldo is one of the most respected old captains on the beach at Coqueiral. He is reputed to know about more fishing spots than anyone else in the village and to have been the most successful fisherman in the area. He has since retired because of a severe case of trachoma, which has seriously affected his sight. Besides being a highly capable fisherman, Mestre Geraldo is a highly inventive man. Although he is unable to read and write, he composes poetry for the local troubadors and lyrics for folk songs and games. He was one of the original founders of the Benevolent Society, and it was under his initiative that the Society undertook the construction of a breeding tank for a supply of bait.

Nevertheless, Sr. Nilo blames Mestre Geraldo for the failure of his fishing boat to take hold. He insists that earnings were good and that only Mestre Geraldo's stubborn adherence to tradition prevented the success of the venture. Mestre Geraldo admits that he earned good money as captain. He also is quick to point out that Sr. Nilo's boat was extremely comfortable, permitting fishermen to stay warm and dry even in the winter. Yet, he chose to leave the boat after eight months and return to his own raft. This occurred during the summer fishing season.

Mestre Geraldo's decision to fish independently was affected in part by Sr. Nilo's attempts to force him to sell his share of the catch to a particular fish hawker. Mestre Geraldo had been selling fish to the same man for several years and felt that it was a binding relationship, which he could not justify breaking. The greater part of his decision, however, was influenced by his earnings. The largest single catch on the boat in the eight-month period was 392 kilos of first-class species of fish, but the fixed prices in Coqueiral clearly limited Mestre Geraldo's profit. He actually was able to earn as much fishing on his own raft in the summer, when he did not have to contend with the share system.

To demonstrate, six men shared half of the 392-kilo catch over a six-day period. Each man earned little more than an average of 5 kilos per day, less what was taken out for home consumption. This came to only slightly more than the 4.5-kilo average catch per day recorded for the *bote à vela* (see Table 9). Since, at intervals, a sailboat must be beached for several days for caulking and general repairs, and fishermen must rest before sailing again, only three voyages a month were made. Even if Mestre Geraldo's crew had caught 392 kilos on every voyage, which they did not, the effects of the share system are such that the fishermen would have had to double their efforts in order to duplicate the earnings from their own *botes*. Mestre Geraldo thus abandoned the sailboat in the summer, hoping to return to it the following winter. Sr. Nilo chose to sell his boat rather than wait out the summer without financial return.

A second hull sailboat belonged to a former president of the fishermen's guild, who moved to the state capital after deciding to sell his boat. Another was owned by Sr. Mario, the secretary of the Benevolent Society, who soon became so incensed by the independence of his captain and crew that he set fire to the craft. The owner of the fourth hull boat to sail from Coqueiral was also its captain, and he kept it going all year round. He alone was responsible and would fish on all possible occasions, regardless of the size of his catch. He was sometimes forced to sail shorthanded or with a less than commendable crew, but he continued to go out until one day he capsized. Afraid to sail again, he sold the boat.

In August, 1965, a fisherman and a fish hawker formed a partnership in order to purchase a hull sailboat that had been beached in the village. The boat, approximately eight meters long and with a closed deck, sold for Cr$300,000 ($166). It was agreed that the fisherman would be captain and that the fish hawker would buy the captain's and the boat's share of the catch for sale at the Guaiamu market. The fisherman combined his earnings from fishing outside of the village on a commercial trawler with his wife's earnings from trading in straw baskets. The fish hawker entered into a complicated series of trade and barter transactions through which he eventually raised Cr$133,000 ($74). He applied Cr$100,000 ($55) to the purchase of the boat and agreed to pay the remainder after several voyages. The owner had originally asked Cr$450,000 ($250) in cash for the boat, but was forced to yield to the lower price of Cr$300,000 and credit terms in order to make the sale. In addition to the agreed-upon price, all repairs, amounting to well over Cr$100,000 ($55), fell on the new owners, but only the fisherman could meet his part of this additional expenditure.

The fish hawker set out to raise his share of the Cr$150,000 ($83) in the following manner. When he entered into the partnership, he had a stock of four pigs, a horse, a mule, some bricks to complete the construction of a house, and a small scale for weighing the fish he bought. He began by selling two pigs for Cr$63,000 ($35), with which he paid a debt of Cr$12,000 ($12) to several of the local storekeepers and to some of his fishermen clientele. He kept the remaining Cr$42,000 ($23) for his daily living expenses and for the purchase of more fish. He then traded his horse for a donkey and the donkey for a radio. He sold his mule for Cr$60,000 ($33) and bought another mule for Cr$80,000 ($44). This he traded in return for a she-ass and Cr$22,000 ($12). The she-ass was exchanged for another donkey, which was also promptly traded off for coconuts, which the fish hawker kept for home consumption. He sold his radio for Cr$47,000 ($26), a pig for Cr$28,000 ($15), and another pig for Cr$20,000 ($11). He traded his bricks for a donkey plus Cr$28,000 ($15). Finally, he sold his scale for Cr$10,000 ($5.50).

He was unable to raise the entire amount needed, however. He therefore held back Cr$33,000 ($18) for daily expenses and for the purchase of fish, and he applied Cr$100,000 ($55) toward the boat. He still owed Cr$50,000 ($27.50) on the purchase price and another $75,000 ($42) for repairs when it set sail for the first time.

When the boat made its maiden voyage, it was desperately in need of a new sail, which the two partners had been unable to buy in Coqueiral. They had completely exhausted all sources of credit and were in considerable debt. After several five-day voyages that brought in under a hundred kilos of fish each time, the boat set sail for Aracajú. It was hoped that catches might be larger around Aracajú or, at least, that whatever fish were caught could be sold at the higher price of Cr$900 ($.50) per kilo. It was also hoped that they might establish credit in Aracajú for the purchase of a sail. The fish hawker remained in Coqueiral to await any remittance of profit. He planned to pay his Cr$50,000 ($27.50) debt for the purchase of the boat out of his profits from the sale of fish. The Cr$75,000 ($42) repair bill, however, he considered as a debt that the boat must pay out of its earnings and not as his personal responsibility.

During the transactions leading up to the purchase of the boat, the local bigwigs insisted that the fisherman and fish hawker would be unable to raise the money to effect the purchase. Both the Colônia de Pescadores and the Benevolent Society rejected the fish hawker's request for a loan. While the boat was undergoing repairs, many of which were made by kinsmen and friends at no cost to the new owners, the local bigwigs would appear at the beach insisting that such labors were in vain. They prided themselves on being able to say that they had "already tried it" and that hull sailboats just would not work. After the boat set sail for Aracajú, they would harass the fish hawker with questions intended to cast doubt on the honesty of his partner. They told him that he would never receive any profits and that he would be lucky to get a letter saying that no fish had been caught. The fish hawker replied that he trusted his colleague. Such talk, he confided later, was proof that the local bigwigs wanted "everything for themselves and wanted the fishermen to have nothing!"

This friction between the local bigwigs and the fishermen is very real. It results from innumerable cases in which self-interested individuals have attempted to take advantage of the fishermen for their own aggrandizement or have tried to prevent fishermen from improving their own lot. The pressures which they bring to bear are sometimes overt, as when Sr. Nilo calls in the police from Guaiamu, and sometimes they are subtle and almost imperceptible. Yet, they are constant and unyielding. There is little that the fishermen themselves can do without the destructive interference of the local bigwigs.

The fate of the Benevolent Society in the hands of the local bigwigs has already been made clear. It has also been mentioned that the Society entertained long-range plans for the construction of a fish pond in an abandoned salt tank for the purpose of breeding shrimp and small fish for bait. It was Mestre Geraldo's idea that bait could be sold to fishermen, whether members of the Society or not, for 10% of the fish caught and sold, and an additional kilo given to the Society for resale. The members of the Society would also have the right to catch all the fish in the tank once a year, at Lent.

The plan for the tank was outlined enthusiastically by Mestre Geraldo. The walls would be built up on all four sides of the tank, and channels would be dug around and across for circulation of the water. Mangrove roots would be removed around the sides of the tank, which would allow for casting the nets. The mangrove swamp would be cut back but part of it left in the center for shade. Mestre Geraldo estimated that his plan could be executed for Cr$200,000 ($110) if the members of the Society would contribute their time and energies.

In July, 1965, upon my recommendation, the Agency for the Development of the Northeast (SUDENE) agreed to provide the necessary funds as an experiment in cooperative activity and in the construction of fish breeding tanks. They approved Mestre Geraldo's plan, and, early in August, a staff member came to Coqueiral to meet with the members of the Society and to turn the money over to the treasurer. Sr. Mario accepted the money in his son's absence and promised to keep an accounting of all expenditures. The money was to be used principally for materials and equipment and to pay a stoneworker; the remainder was to pay for day labor to dig out the tank.

The members of the Benevolent Society realized that the SUDENE funds would only give initial impulse to the project. They agreed among themselves to apply the interest earned from loans and their own labor toward the completion of the tank once the money had run out. The man in charge, Mestre Geraldo, calculated the expenses and immediately began to work as a hired laborer, earning Cr$1,000 ($.55) per day. Sr. Mario and the president of the Society, claiming that it was necessary for them to serve in an administrative function, offered to pay laborers to do their share of the work. They set out to buy the materials needed for the construction of the tank and to contract a stoneworker to lay the concrete foundation for the floodgate. Until the tidewater was cut off from the tank it was impossible to begin the work in earnest.

Sr. Mario's first official act was to buy a board that was salvaged from the boat to which he had set fire ten years before. He paid himself Cr$5,000 ($2.70) for the charred piece of wood, which was to be cut down for use as the flood gate. The president delivered sacks of cement, sand, and rocks to the site in his horse-drawn cart for Cr$7,500 ($4.10). The equivalent of twelve and one-half days' worth of labor had been spent in the first few hours on services rendered by the Society's own board of directors.

Sr. Mario and the president justified charges for services to their own Society on the premise that someone would have earned the money anyway. Under fire they agreed, in principle, to return these funds to the Society's coffers. When it was also suggested that they contribute their share of the labor for the building of the tank and that the absentee treasurer's 20% earnings on interest be cut, both men renounced their positions on the board. The secretary also resigned from the Society, while the ex-president remained a member. Neither returned their earnings from the SUDENE funds. Three members of the Society, frightened by the upheaval, also quit after withdrawing their share of monthly contributions.

Sr. Mario had "dragged his feet," and it was not until well into September that he finally arranged for a stoneworker. By late September, when he resigned, the floodgate had been erected and some of the digging begun. By mid-October, the SUDENE funds were exhausted. Besides the cost of materials and equipment plus the salary of the stoneworker, some seventy days of paid labor had been quickly used up by ambitious villagers. The remaining members of the Society agreed to continue their work, dividing the area to be dug into twelve-meter plots. A plot was assigned to each of the eleven members. Those who were too old or sick to work in the mangrove swamp promised to hire labor at an established rate of Cr$400 ($.22) per meter. For many of the retired fishermen this meant spending Cr$4,800 ($2.60) out of their Cr$26,000 ($14) monthly pension. Although the members demonstrated their will to complete the tank, much of the delay up to this point had been owing to their age and their inability to work effectively in the mangrove swamp. The mud and roots made the digging slow and tedious. The hindrance of the tides and mosquitos also helped to slow the progress of the work. Nevertheless, by the end of October, each of the members had done his part of the work on the tank, which was then about three-fourths complete.

By far the most detrimental effect on the work of the Society came from the presence of those board members whose primary interest was their own personal enrichment. Although the Society was founded in reaction against the family which had tightly controlled the Colônia de Pescadores for over twenty years, its members were forced to invite politically interested parties from the opposition. Only when the secretary and the president resigned from the Society did the serious work on the fish tank begin. Their main objective had not been the construction of the fish tank nor the careful use of SUDENE funds.

Rather, their interest lay in discovering how much of the SUDENE funds could be diverted to their own use and how much political advantage they might derive from the Society. Since the fish tank was an experiment that could have failed, they preferred to disassociate themselves from it. They neither joined in the work themselves nor encouraged other members of the Society to work.

With the work well advanced on the fish tank, the Society received an additional Cr$200,000 ($110) from SUDENE. Mestre Geraldo was elevated to president. He requested and received the aid of a literate *compadre*, one of the owners of the remaining salt tanks, in the keeping of records and books. This *compadre* also kept the money locked in a trunk in his home. In his new role as president, Mestre Geraldo has maintained a high level of interest in the Society. He has kept a core of retired fishermen hard at work to complete the fish tank. With the promise of help from his literate *compadre* and with SUDENE's supervision, there was no need for him to involve leaders of either political group in the county. Energies could be directed exclusively toward completion of the fish tank and toward consolidation of an association comprised of fishermen sharing common needs and goals.

In 1967 I returned to Coqueiral to find a defunct Benevolent Society and a badly organized and malfunctioning fish breeding tank. SUDENE funds had been used up in the completion of the tank, and there was no money available for its upkeep and maintenance. The old men were evidently weary of toiling in the mud; without the representatives of SUDENE to encourage them, they gave way to the remonstrations of the local bigwigs. The mangrove swamp grew up again, overrunning the tank.

[X]

Conclusion

IN THIS STUDY I have examined the processes of change within the traditional raft fishing economy of Northeast Brazil by means of historical, economic, and sociological investigation. This analytical approach follows from my conviction that peasant decision-making and subsequent behavior are conditioned by the *complex* interplay of ecological, social, structural, and organizational factors which comprise the totality of that domain known as the peasant economy.

In the preceding chapters I have tried to elaborate those factors that affect the outcome of decisions concerning the acceptance or rejection of technological innovations. It should be clear from the foregoing account that the peasant economy is not an easily bounded sub-system, and that a variety of forces form the alternatives from which the peasant fisherman makes his choices. Although the locus of peasant economic life is the family, and it is within the household that most decisions are made and acted upon, socioeconomic relationships extend far beyond the limits of the household or even the community. Since traditional economies are part economies which serve among other things as commodity producers for a larger system, household decisions depend upon events in the wider universe, many of them beyond the immediate control of the peasant fisherman. Therefore, we must approach the subject of innovation and change in peasant societies in two ways. On the one hand, we must understand the quality of household relationships and the extended family ties that sustain the local economy. On the other hand, we must examine the exchange relationships which exist in the larger ecological complex and which clearly account for peasant behavior.

An alternative approach in the anthropological literature is presented by George Foster, who posits for the members of every society a "common cognitive orientation" from which behavior is derived. According to Foster, "The model of cognitive orientation that seems best to *account for* (emphasis mine) peasant behavior is the 'Image of Limited Good'" (1965:296).[1] That is,

. . . peasants view their social, economic, and natural universe—their total environment—as one in which all of the desired things in life such as land, wealth, health, friendship and love, manliness and honor, respect and status, power and influence, security and safety, exist in finite quantity and are always in short supply as far as the peasant is concerned. Not only do these and all other "good things" exist in finite and limited quantities, but in addition there is no way directly within peasant power to increase the available quantities (*Ibid.*, 296).

While Foster may be giving us an adequate description of the ethos of the Mexican village where his research was done, his thesis treats only a part of a system which he attempts to view as closed and from within (*Ibid.*). In his rather "ontological" approach to the existence of peasant communities,[2] he fails to explain the cultural phenomenon of peasant conservatism as a result of historically given power relationships that provide the peasant with his "rules of the game of living." Although he footnotes his recognition that peasant communities are parts of more complex societies (*Ibid.*, 311), he does not seem to think that the "symbiotic spatial-temporal relationships," about which he wrote earlier (1953:163), are necessary to an understanding of the attitudes and values held by the villagers. In this way, he clearly forgoes the analytical framework that I believe necessary for an understanding of peasant conservatism. There can be little doubt that the peasant's desires are not finite and that the possibility of fulfilling them are not in his own hands (Nash 1964:226; De Vries 1961:43).

Given this assumption, it is essential for us to understand the role of local elites as mediators between the peasant and the wider system in which he participates. In Coqueiral, it is the local bigwigs who manipulate the natural and social environments to their own ends. In their attempt to exploit the labor of peasant fishermen, they exacerbate the tensions that prevail in the village, an incipiently stratified local community in which superordinate-subordinate relationships are maintained by virtue of the bigwigs' access to outside sources of wealth and power—notably, the sugar producers and coconut planters desirous of a steady supply of inexpensive high-quality fish.

These local bigwigs dominate the daily life of the peasant fishermen in an effort to serve their own interests. They dictate codes of conduct and enforce legislation designed to control the prices and marketing of fish. It is they who introduced hull sailboats to Coqueiral in order to enrich themselves by exacting as their share one-half of the catch from fishermen who, as permanent crew members, would become, in effect, sharecroppers-at-sea. At the same time, the bigwigs discouraged the introduction of other techniques, such as the gill nets, which might provide capital, and thus mobility, to the fishermen.

Yet, within the limits set by their ecosystem, the peasant fishermen remain free to select the fishing strategy most advantageous for their own economic well-being and to accept innovations that maximize their individual gain—as is evidenced, for example, in the widespread use of new, more efficient nets. Despite the introduction of the larger hull sailboats, the fishermen of Coqueiral show a preference for the traditional log rafts, which indicates a more general preference for independent production.

The alternation of fishing pattern between independent production and fishing as the member of a crew on someone else's raft represents a highly rational adaptation to local ecological conditions that took place long before the introduction of hull sailboats. Jangadeiros maximize their own productive efforts by using several types of rafts equipped to exploit a variety of fisheries. The added comfort of hull sailboats makes it possible for fishermen to spend longer stretches of time at sea, but their range is still limited to fishing above the continental shelf, and handlining from sailboats in the same general area exploited by jangadas does not increase the daily catch per man. Instead, hook-and-line fishing from hull sailboats extends the hours and energy spent fishing without altering the work-production ratio in any significant way. Even more important, the share system requires that a fisherman devote twice the numbers of hours to earn the same amount of money he obtains as an independent producer because he must contribute half of his fish to the nonfishing owner of the boat. While changes in boat type might be accompanied by considerable increases in over-all production by joining a number of men together

in the fishing process over longer periods, few if any benefits accrue
to the fishermen, owing to the disproportionate share of the catch
taken by the owner of the vessel.

Moreover, market controls in turn affect production strategies.
Fishermen have a clear understanding of the way in which the market
functions. They are aware of the difference between a "free" and a
controlled market because they have received far higher prices for
their fish in urban markets, where the rigid price ceilings that characterize the local Market Place are not in effect. They are cognizant, too,
of the extent of consumer demands, and the alternation of fishing
pattern within given seasons is predicated on the receptivity of the
market. Given the price controls in Coqueiral and the dangers of a
saturated market, there is little monetary incentive to fish on hull
sailboats.

In sum, as long as the logs necessary for the construction of rafts are
available and within their means, and while the local market structure
continues to be prohibitive, jangadeiros will have no incentive to alter
their traditional fishing pattern. Generally speaking, where there have
been rewards for hard work, motivations will be high, and the level of
performance will stay constant and perhaps rise. Where there is no
notion that increased work pays off, however, there will be limited
aspirations—simply to maintain past levels of achievement—rather
than increased incentives to hard work or innovation.

The peasant fisherman in Northeast Brazil sees a definite relationship between wealth, production techniques, and work.[3] He is also
aware that there can be no further accumulation of wealth *for him*
with the production techniques available to him *no matter how hard
he works*. In fact, the jangadeiro sees his fishing universe as being infinitely expandable given new production techniques. He knows that
nets are likely to yield a larger catch than hooks and line and that
motorized vessels could open up new fishing grounds. However, new
techniques and technology cannot be acquired arbitrarily. Some advantage must accrue to the peasant before he will accept innovations.

It is the entrepreneur wanting to exploit an enlarged market who in-
troduces new techniques, and these are *rationally accepted or rejected
by a people with freedom of choice*. There is always discussion of
alternatives and of economic advantage among peasant producers

(Firth 1964:22). There is also widespread knowledge of market conditions and production costs and a strong desire to maximize returns for productive efforts (Bauer and Yamey 1957:96-97). Differential acceptance or rejection of innovations does not necessarily reflect the lack of motivation which is all too often attributed to peasants. Rather, the dangers for a marginal earner with limited capital can be very great, and experimentation among peasants occurs only when the risk is low. As Firth (1961:109) points out, the peasant ". . . has a highly expandable set of wants." *The overwhelming problem is his limited means.*

Fishermen have been able to maintain their status as independent producers in the face of the rising cost of logs by combining their own efforts with those of members of their families and by the cooperation of their fellow jangadeiros. Indeed, while disputing neither the individuality of the fisherman nor the amount of interpersonal strife in rural villages, one must emphasize that intrafamilial—and even interfamilial—cooperation is essental to the maintenance of the most traditional peasant economies. The community of Coqueiral functions, through the cooperation of its members, to the best advantage of the individual and his household. In order to accumulate the capital necessary to replace log rafts and/or their parts, the fishermen depend upon income from diverse household occupations, including animal husbandry and straw handicrafts. Economic risk is offset not only by the diversification of economic roles within a family, but also by the large number of people engaging in any single occupation. Hence, the large number of middlemen created by agreements between individual fishermen and fish hawkers, who are often kinsmen, tends to distribute the risks inherent in an easily glutted market evenly throughout the village.

At the same time, a system of credit and savings exists through the workings of these extended families. This system serves to maintain the traditional economy rather than to afford significant sums of money for investment in innovations. In fact, the need to insulate these carefully balanced productive and banking units against the dangers of risk often inhibits innovation. Peasant societies operate so near to the bare margin of existence that the security of the individual becomes one with the security of the group. It is an attempt to protect his security rather than a distaste for sharing (Bauer and Yamey 1057:103 *et passim*) that leads the peasant producer to reject innovations.[4]

There is an obvious need to examine closely the nature of cooperation and competition in traditional societies, particularly as these factors are related to social mobility and change.[5] I have noted the high degree of cooperation among peasants within the general fishing economy in Coqueiral and hypothesized that economic competition between individual productive units is actually minimized by the maintenance of secrecy about fishing spots. Peasants do not jockey for position against each other, and intravillage hostilities are more often than not generated by noneconomic factors. Competition seems rather to characterize behavior among the local bigwigs, whose mobility is often gained at the expense of their fellows. Not only do they seek control over the fishermen's labor for their own profit, but they are also intent on perpetuating an ideology of superiority as a crucial indicator of their rank to outside sources of power. Thus, the bigwigs consistently denigrate the beliefs and values of peasant fishermen and ridicule the fishermen's attempts to improve their situation. They vie for status and prestige in the eyes of the landowning "power-holders" in the region, thereby gaining access to resources not available to the rest of the local peasantry. They invest these resources in innovations that will help them to stabilize their own position in the local socioeconomic system, and not in ways that are likely to benefit the community as a whole.

Commenting upon the possibility of economic change and growth, Foster (1965:309) argues that David McClelland's psychological prescription—"the need for Achievement," or, n Achievement (McClelland 1953, 1961)[6]—is not lacking in peasant society but lies suppressed beneath the surface by the sanctions of traditional villagers, who, in the spirit of "limited good," discourage personal initiative. He then offers a simple instruction—to wit: change the opportunity structure by opening the "system" and a fertile field for the full expression of n Achievement will be propagated. But this merely lays bare the complexity of the problem and hardly approaches a solution. The solution must lie instead in an explanation of those factors in the ecological and social system from which peasant cognitive orientations are formed.

Brazilian peasants do not lack initiative. Rather, it is clear that entrepreneurship exists at all levels of Brazilian society. The multiplicity of middlemen active in the market arena attests to this fact (Forman and Riegelhaupt 1970). Whether or not entrepreneurship comes to the surface, however, depends wholly on the possibilities for its expression and development. It is important to explain how entrepreneurs emerge and why at a given time.[7] If the underlying socioeconomic system does not permit of capital formation within the local economy, we will not find effective entrepreneurship arising out of the peasant sector no matter how much initiative peasants might have. On the other hand, if there is not a market for goods, there will be no outside entrepreneurial investment at the local level no matter how much creative genius and business acumen exist in the society at large.

By focusing attention on these sociological and economic factors I do not mean to imply that psychological and social psychological phenomena do not play a part in technological innovation. There are motivational differences among individuals. However, a psychological level of analysis does not provide satisfactory causal explanations of innovation and change. It is my belief that obstacles to change in peasant societies are not so much psychological and cognitive as they are ecological and social. Lack of development in the peasant sector is not owing to inherent limitations in a closed system nor to the peasant's inability to cooperate or to perceive possible alternative courses of action. Rather, it is owing to politico-socioeconomic factors beyond the peasant's control.

Observation and informants' statements clearly indicate that class consciousness has a decisive influence on achievement motivation in Brazil.[8] Peasants are well aware of the nature of the bonds which tie them to the dominant segments of society and which clearly limit their mobility. They think in terms of "we and they" and "everything for them, nothing for us." They contrast themselves to the rich and the powerful and fear that they themselves are "nothing in this world." When queried as to why they do not try to improve their situation, they correctly cite lack of opportunity: *"Não tem possibilidades!"* They know there is nothing inherent in their poverty, and they always hope to rise above it. If we can delineate one common peasant thought, then surely it is the overwhelming desire to rid themselves of the yoke of poverty and to share in all the good things with which the twentieth century tempts them.

The so-called "traditional barriers to change" have been erected over the past four centuries by socioeconomic conditions far beyond the control of peasants. Shown an effective way to improve their situation, peasants will readily accept innovation and change. As we have seen, such "effective ways" may well require a complete restructuring of local society (and beyond). The ideology of an inherent peasant conservatism has existed far too long as a rationalization for the exploitation of man. We can no longer justify the immobilizing effects of widespread poverty by our own conservative thoughts regarding peasant behavior. If social scientists are to contribute to an understanding of the processes of change in traditional societies, we must place our discussions of peasant decision-making firmly within a comprehensive framework that includes the ecological and social-structural parameters which condition peasant behavior.

Bibliography

Albuquerque, Orlando de A.
  1961 Noticias sôbre a economica pesquiera da Amazonia. Rio de
        Janeiro: Ministério da Agricultura.
Almeida Prado, J. F. de
  1941 Pernambuco e as capitanias do norte do Brasil (1530-1630).
        Tomo II. Rio de Janeiro: Brasiliana.
Altavilla, Jayme de
  1933 Historia de civilisação das Alagoas. Maceió.
Alves Camara, Antônio
  1888 Ensaio sôbre as construcções Navaes Indigenas do Brasil. Rio de
        Janeiro.
Antão de Carvalho, Vicente
  1962 "Pesca do xareu na Bahia e sua tradição histórica." Revista
        Nacional de Pesca 18:29-37.
Bauer, Peter T., and Basil S. Yamey
  1957 The Economics of Under-developed Countries. Chicago: Uni-
        versity of Chicago Press.
Bennett, John W.
  1966 "Further Remarks on Foster's 'Image of Limited Good.'"
        American Anthropologist 68:206-209.
Bernardes, Lysia Maria Cavalcanti
  1959 "Pescadores da ponta do Cajú: aspectos da contribuição de Por-
        tugueses e Espanhóis para o desenvolvimento da pesca na Guana-
        bara." Revista Brasileira de Geografia 2:24-49.
Bottomanne, C. J.
  1959 Principles of Fisheries Development. Amsterdam: North Hol-
        land Publishing Company.
Brandão, Ambrôsio Fernandes
  n.d. Diálogos das Grandezas do Brasil. Rio de Janeiro: Academia de
        Letras do Brasil (1930).

140   BIBLIOGRAPHY

Brandão, J. M.
   1964   "Glossário de nomes dos peixes: português, inglês, sistemático."
        Boletim de Estudos de Pesca 4:11-40.
Camara Cascudo, Luís de
   1957a   *Jangada*. Rio de Janeiro: Ministério da Educação e Cultura.
   1957b   *Jangadeiros*. Rio de Janeiro: Ministério de Educação e Cultura.
César de Magalhães
   1966   "Jangada e jangadeiros no Brasil." *Fatos e Fotos* 28:2-9.
Coelho, Ranylson R.
   1963   "Aspectos bio-technológicos da pesca marinha no Maranhão,
        Piauí, e Ceará." *Boletim de Estudos de Pesca* 3:8-18.
Comitas, Lambros E.
   1962   "Fishermen and Cooperation in Rural Jamaica." Ph.D. disserta-
        tion, Columbia University.
Correia de Andrade, Manuel
   1959   *Os Rios Coruripe, Jiquiá, e São Miguel*. Vol. 4 of *Os rios-do-
        açucar do nordeste oriental*. Recife: Instituto Joaquim Nabuco
        de Pesquisas Sociais.
Costa, Francisco Izidoro Rodrigues
   1901   "Descrição geográfica, estatística e histórica dos municípios do
        estado de Alagoas." *Revista do Instituto Arqueológico e Geo-
        gráfico Alagoano*, vol 8.
Cruz, João Francisco de e Melquiades Pinto Paiva
   1964   *Sôbre a biologia da albacora, Thunnus atlanticus, no nordeste
        Brasileira*. Rio Grande do Norte: Instituto de Biologia Marinha.
Cunha de Azevedo Coutinho, J. J.
   1801   *A Political Essay on the Commerce of Portugal and Her Col-
        onies, Particularly of Brazil in South America*. London.
Davidson, Stanley, A. P. Meikeljohn, and R. Passmore
   1959   *Human Nutrition and Dietetics*. Edinburgh: E. & S. Livingstone
        Ltd.
De Vries, Egbert
   1961   *Man in Rapid Social Change*. Garden City, New York: Double-
        day & Co.
Documentos Históricos do Arquivo Municipal.
   1625-1629   Salvador: Prefeitura Municipal do Salvador.
Domingues, Alfredo José P.
   1962   "Aspectos fisicos do meio-norte e do nordeste." In *Passagens do
        Brasil*. Rio de Janeiro: Instituto Brasileiro de Geografia e Estatís-
        tica, pp. 171-181.

Espindola, Thomaz do Bom-Fim
   1871   *Geographia Alagoana ou descripão physico, político, e histórica da provincia das Alagoas.* Maceió: Typographia do Liberal.
Firth, Raymond
   1946   *Malay Fishermen: Their Peasant Economy.* London.
   1961   *Elements of Social Organization.* London: Watts & Co.
   1964   "Capital, Saving and Credit in Peasant Societies: A Viewpoint from Economic Anthropology." In Raymond Firth and B. S. Yamey, eds., *Capital, Saving and Credit in Peasant Societies.* London: George Allen & Unwin, Ltd. pp. 15-34.
Forman, Shepard
   1964   "The Location of Fishing Spots in a Brazilian Coastal Village." Unpublished ms.
Forman, Shepard, and Joyce F. Riegelhaupt
   1970   "Market Place and Marketing System: Toward a Theory of Peasant Economic Integration." *Comparative Studies in Society and History* 12 (2): 188-212.
Foster, George M.
   1953   "What is Folk Culture?" *American Anthropologist* 55:159-173.
   1960   *Culture and Conquest: America's Spanish Heritage.* Viking Fund Publication in Anthropology No. 27, New York.
   1962   *Traditional Cultures and the Impact of Technological Change.* New York: Harper & Row.
   1965   "Peasant Society and the Image of Limited Good." *American Anthropologist* 67:293-315.
   1966   "Reply to Kaplan, Saler and Bennett." *American Anthropologist* 68:210-214.
Fraser, Thomas M.
   1960   *Rusembilan: A Malay Fishing Village in Southern Thailand.* Ithaca: Cornell University Press.
Freyre, Gilberto
   1963   *The Mansions and the Shanties.* Translated by Harriet de Onis. New York: Alfred A. Knopf.
Furtado, Celso
   1963   *The Economic Growth of Brazil.* Berkeley: University of California Press.
Gordon, H. Scott
   1954   "The Economic Theory of the Common Property Resource: The Fishery." *Journal of Political Economy* 62:124-142.

Grant, Andrew
   1809   *History of Brazil*. London.

Hammel, E. A., and Ynez D. Haase
   n.d.   "A Survey of Peruvian Fishing Communities." *University of California Anthropology Records* 21:2. Berkeley and Los Angeles: University of California Press.

Herald, Earl Stannard
   1961   *Living Fishes of the World*. Garden City, New York: Doubleday & Co.

Indicador Geral do Estado de Alagoas
   1902   *Relatório*. Maceió: T. Ramalho & Murta.

Institute of Nutrition of Central America (INCAP) and the Interdepartmental Committee on Nutrition for National Defense (ICNND).
   1961   *Food Composition Table for Use in Latin America*. Bethesda, Maryland: National Institutes of Health.

Iria, Alberto
   1956   *Descobrimentos portugeses*. 2 vols. Lisbon: Institute de Alto Cultura.

James, Preston
   1959   *Latin America*. New York: Odyssey Press.

Kaplan, David, and Benson Saler
   1966   " 'Foster's Image of Limited Good': An Example of Anthropological Explanation." *American Anthropologist* 68:202-205.

Kennedy, John G.
   1966   "Peasant Society and the Image of Limited Good: A Critique." *American Anthropologist* 68:1212-1225.

Kottak, Conrad Phillip
   1966   "The Structure of Equality in a Brazilian Fishing Community." Ph.D. dissertation, Columbia University.

Lagos, Paulo Fernando de
   1961   "Contribução geográfico ao estudo da pesca em Santa Catarina." *Revista Brasileira de Geografia* 1:212-215.

McClelland, David C.
   1953   *The Achievement Motive*. New York: Appleton-Century-Crofts, Inc.
   1961   *The Achieving Society*. Princeton, New Jersey: D. Van Nostrand Co., Inc.

Maio, Celeste Rodrigues
   1962   "Relevo e estrutura: litoral." In *Grandes regiões meionorte e*

nordeste. Rio de Janeiro: Instituto Brasileiro de Geografia e Estatística, pp. 9-73.

Murphy, Robert E.
1964 "Social Change and Acculturation." *Transactions of the New York Academy of Sciences.* 26:845-854.

Nash, Manning
1964 "Social Prerequisites to Economic Growth in Latin America and Southeast Asia." *Economic Development and Culture Change* 12:225-242.

Oberg, Kalervo
1965 "The Marginal Peasant in Brazil." *American Anthropologist* 67:1417-1427.

Paiva, Melquiades Pinto
1959 "Exploração da lagosta no Ceará." *Seleções agrícolas* 14:41-42.

Piker, Steven
1966 " 'The Image of Limited Good:' Comments on an Exercise in Description and Interpretation." *American Anthropologist* 68:1202-1211.

Richards, P. W.
1952 *The Tropical Rain Forest.* Cambridge: Cambridge University Press.

Richardson, I. D.
1962 "Survey of Brazilian Fishing Grounds." *Fishing News International* 1 (4): 42-44.

Rosen, Bernard C.
1962 "Socialization Process and Achievement Motivation." *American Sociological Review* 27:612-624.
1964 "The Achievement Syndrome and Economic Growth in Brazil." *Social Forces* 42:341-353.

Russell, E. S.
1942 *The Overfishing Problem.* Cambridge: Cambridge University Press.

Siegel, Bernard J.
1955 "Social Structure and Economic Change in Brazil." In Simon Kuznets, Wilbert E. Moore, and Joseph J. Spengler, eds., *Economic Growth: Brazil, India, China.* Durham, North Carolina: Duke University Press, pp. 388-411.

Smith, T. Lynn
1963 *Brazil: People and Institutions.* Baton Rouge: Louisiana State University Press.

Soares de Sousa, Gabriel
  1587   *Tratado descriptiva do Brasil em 1587*. São Paulo (1938).
Stanislawski, Dan
  1963   *Portugal's Other Kingdom, the Algarve*. Austin: University of Texas Press.
Swift, M. G.
  1964   "Capital, Saving and Credit in a Malay Peasant Economy." In Raymond Firth and B. S. Yamey, eds., *Capital, Saving and Credit in Peasant Societies*. London: George Allen & Unwin Ltd.
Verdonck, Adriaen
  1630   "Memoria apresentada ao conselho político do Brasil em 30 de Maio de 1630." *Revista Archeológico e Geográfico de Pernambuco* 55(1901):215-227.
Vilhena, Luiz Santos
  1802   *Recopilação de noticias soterpolitanas e Brasilicas*. Bahia (1921).
Wagley, Charles
  1963   *Introduction to Brazil*. New York: Columbia University Press.
Wagley, Charles, and Marvin Harris
  1955   "A Typology of Latin American Subcultures." *American Anthropologist* 57:426-451.
Waibel, Leo
  1949   "Principios da colonização no sul do Brasil." *Revista Brasileira de Geografia* 2 (2): 159-222.
Waterlow, J., and A. Vergara
  1956   *Protein Malnutrition in Brazil*. New York, Rome: Food and Agriculture Organization (FAO) of the United Nations.
Wilson, Eva D., Katherine H. Fisher, and Mary E. Fuqua
  1959   *Principles of Nutrition*. New York: John Wiley & Sons.
Wolf, Eric R.
  1966   *Peasants*. Englewood Cliffs, New Jersey: Prentice-Hall, Inc.
Wynne-Edwards, Vero Copner
  1962   *Animal Dispersion in Relation to Social Behavior*. New York: Hafner Publishing Co.

Notes

I. INTRODUCTION

1. The rate of exchange in the year 1965–66 was approximately Cr$1,800-US$1. Cr$ is the standard notation for *cruzeiro*, the unit of Brazilian currency; where it appears in the text the comparable US$ value will be noted in parentheses.

2. The sails were introduced in the seventeenth century by the Portuguese (Camara Cascudo 1957a:90).

3. Following Firth (1964:17), the word "peasant" refers to a "socio-economic system of small-scale producers with a relatively simple, non-industrial technology." The system is essentially rural and depends upon the existence of a market. According to Firth (*Ibid.*, 18), the concept involves a "set of structural and social relationships rather than a technological category of persons engaged in the same employment . . ." As such, a peasant is a peasant not because of the kind of work he does but because of the visible set of relationships which bind him to a larger system. Wolf (1966:11 *et passim*) defines "peasantry" as a part system tied to a larger universe in which the role the peasant is to act out is strictly defined. His dependency is manifest in part by the payment of a *fund of rent* to someone who stands in a superordinate position (*Ibid.*, 8). Fishermen are structurally and functionally akin to agricultural producers vis-à-vis the larger society of which each is a part. Fishermen also pay a fund of rent, either in the form of a share of the catch or in a regular percentage paid to local branches of the national fishermen's guild. See Firth (1946) for the classic study of a peasant fishing economy. It should be noted that Firth is not specifically interested in problems of technological innovation and change, but in the nature of the peasant society itself.

4. An essay on Portuguese commerce with Brazil in 1801 states that Indians were *more inclined* to fishing than were Africans. It suggests that: "It would be useful to lay a tax on every black, who is a fisherman or a sailor, and, on the other hand, to confer a bounty on every owner of a net or ship, whose servants are all native Indians" (Cunha de Azevedo 1801:55). Camara Cascudo (1957a:26) affirms that some slaves did fish on jangadas, but as members of the crew and never as captains.

145

5. A series of litigations involving nucleated communities located on privately owned plantations has taken place in Brazil. One such case is that of Praia de Forte in the state of Bahia (Kottak 1966:262).

6. These techniques were introduced into Portugal by the Phoenicians around 1000 B.C. (Stanislawski 1963:88–89).

7. The lower cost of the smaller *saveiros* used in the Bahia area brings them within reach of all fishermen (Kottak:1966) and probably accounts for the more equitable share system (one-fourth rather than one-half) which prevails in the region. Fishing at the turn of the nineteenth century in Bahia was characterized by a number of large vessels owned by a relatively few individuals and functioning under a one-half share system (Grant 1809:178). The change to a more equitable share system would have been necessary to attract a permanent crew in cases where individual ownership of small craft was readily possible.

II. THE COMMUNITY: COQUEIRAL

1. Since this study was to deal with the factor of human choice, it was necessary that harbor conditions of the chosen site not preclude the possibility of a change from rafts to hull sailboats.

2. At least one Brazilian historian contends that this was the first point sighted by Cabral in 1500 (Altavilla 1933:7).

3. The name of the county, Guaiamu, is the Tupi word for the species of crab *(Cardisoma guanhami)* which is so abundant in the mangrove swamp.

4. Almeida Prado (1941) points out that a highway which ran along the coast of Alagoas through Guaiamu from Olinda to the São Francisco River community of Penedo existed at this time.

5. The fact that cargo vessels were constructed in Coqueiral indicates that there were skilled craftsmen capable of making hull sailboats instead of the rafts which traditionally have been used in fishing.

6. "The lands more or less concentrated adjacent to the sea as well as those bordering on all woodlands judged to be useless for the Royal navy will be set aside for the agriculture of the people." (Vilhena 1921:804–805).

7. The tableland stretching from Coqueiral to the neighboring village of Lagôa Sêca, in the north, is covered with potsherds and ceramic pieces from tile roofs. There are many reports of *aldeias de caboclo*, or villages of pacified Indians, in the area. The manufacture of lime has virtually destroyed the *sambaquis*, or shell mounds, which were reputed to cover the area. The author did discover a pot identified as Caeté by Dr. Theo Brandão, Faculdade de Filosofia, Universidade de Alagoas.

8. Waibel (1949) estimates that a family of five to seven people needs

five hectares under cultivation in order to maintain a subsistence level of living (Oberg 1965:1425).

9. Depending on market conditions, these figures represent high and low prices in a given year (1965).

10. "*Município* is an administrative subdivision of the state roughly comparable to the county in the United States. It consists of one *cidade* and the surrounding territory. It may or may not be subdivided into *distritos do paz*, each centered about a *vila*" (T. Lynn Smith 1963:635).

11. A bronze factory which manufactured church bells for the entire province of Pernambuco is said to have existed in Guaiamu in 1871 (Espindola 1871:236–37). There was no industry in the county capital as of 1965.

12. The seasons are not distinguished by any great variance in temperature. The summer, however, is usually clear and calm, while winter refers to the rainy season, often accompanied by wind and turblent waters.

III. SOCIAL STRUCTURE AND THE PEASANT ECONOMY

1. Two descendents of traditional local elites remain in Coqueiral. They own and operate the two remaining salt tanks in the village. Both own a few coconut trees. Their income from salt production is lower than that of the local bigwigs. While they maintain amiable relations with the fishermen, they refuse to take part in local politics. A number of sugar planters from the valley spend their summers in Coqueiral, but they have little effect on the local economy. They buy some fish during the summer season and Lenten period. At best, a few of them supply logs for rafts in return for fish. One of them loaned money to a fisherman for the purchase of a nylon gill net. Their primary interest, however, is in a supply of fish, and they leave the day-to-day dealings with the fishermen to the local bigwigs.

2. It is unlikely that the traditional rural political system of ruling oligarchies will be affected in any way by the Brazilian military government's decree of 1964 abolishing political parties and reforming them under one government and one opposition party.

3. The traditional elites are not fully aware of the tensions which exist between the local bigwigs and the peasant since they tend to lump them all together. They are aware of the poverty of the lower classes and, generally, show good intentions when speaking about the peasants' problems. The owners of the sugar mill have initiated a series of social reforms on their lands. There is, however, still a tendency to romanticize poverty, especially in the idyllic setting of Coqueiral. (See also the chapter on "Social Classes" in Wagley 1963:99–147.)

4. This land, located within thirty-eight meters of the high-tide mark, is actually the property of the federal government.

5. The villagers claim that Sr. Nilo's acquisition of wealth came from the sale of merchandise from a large merchant vessel which was torpedoed off the coast of Guaiamu in the early years of World War II.

6. It is not known what percentage of the farm is owned by Sr. Nilo and what percentage belongs to his brother-in-law, who spends full time at the farm.

7. Sr. Nilo's party carried the county in a statewide election in 1965, and the village of Coqueiral, by a small margin. There is evidence, however, that members of the fishermen's guild voted overwhelmingly for the opposition candidate.

8. One worked as a brick layer and the other two as tailors in Guaiamu before the post was built. A fourth brother migrated to Rio de Janeiro, where he is a mechanic. Although the nurse has no medical training, he once performed breast surgery on a fisherman's wife. Submission of this sort to the abusive use of local power is far from uncommon in the Brazilian hinterland.

9. This system has historic roots in the supplying of fish to sugar plantations for the satisfaction of masters and the sustenance of slaves (Freyre 1963:161).

10. The roots of the *colônias* can be found in the medieval guilds of thirteenth-century Spain and Portugal (Iria 1956:86, 224–25 *et passim*).

11. It is likely that a religious brotherhood formerly existed in Coqueiral and was supplanted by the Colônia.

IV. STRATIFICATION AND PRODUCTIVE TECHNOLOGY

1. Beach seines depended on the use of slave labor in pre-abolition Brazil. Slaves divided their time between the coast and the plantation for the alternate harvests (Antão de Carvalho 1962:32–33).

2. "The smooth dog is not considered an edible species, and the sports fisherman finds it uninteresting. Its one contribution to mankind is its abundance, providing an adequate supply for classroom dissection and study" (Herald 1961:25). It is commonly eaten, however, by residents along the northeast coast of Brazil.

V. THE NATURE OF RAFT FISHING

1. No English translation was found for this species, although the species is listed in Brandão (1964).

2. This kind of fishing is called the *pescaria "dirivim,"* a contraction of *"de ir e vir"* (to go and to come).

3. Similar systems of named fishing grounds and landmarks and the secrecy of particular spots are reported for the entire northeast coast of

Brazil (Camara Cascudo 1957a:22–25, 1957b:5–6, Forman 1964, César de Magalhães 1966:2, Kottak 1966:163–64). However, these phenomena seem to be far more generalized among fishermen the world over. According to a personal communication from Dr. E. Lowe Pierce, Department of Zoology, University of Florida, "This type of position-finding is an old method with fishermen, and it is also probably an even older custom not to reveal your best fishing spots to your fellow competitors."

4. While all informants interviewed agreed on the names of the fishing grounds as outlined in Map III, names and locations of fishing spots within these differed according to informant.

5. Carl O. Schweidenbank, Marine Biology Laboratory, Woods Hole, Massachusetts, states in a personal communication: "I believe that you will find that they [the fishermen] are correct in using visual marks for fishing in any given spot. We have found that fixed objects on shore are much better and certainly more accurate than radar or fathometers. We have used this method ourselves . . . in dredging for certain species of fish in different localities." Dr. Marta Vannucci of the Oceanographic Institute, Universidade de São Paulo, reports in a personal communication that experiments with fishermen in the waters around the Island of Fernand de Noronha indicated that they were able to return to the same location time and again with a surprising degree of accuracy.

6. Fish are not believed to be sedentary, and their habitats are clearly associated with seasonal and even daily climatic variations. Some attention is given to feeding habits. The same species of fish is known to be found at widely varying depths and above both rocky and gravel bottoms. Fish are known to migrate over great distances, and species associated with fresh water are sometimes found in ocean areas. Fishermen relate this latter phenomenon directly to the silting up of the bay in the winter months by the waters from the rivers to the south.

7. According to Schweidenbank (personal communication), "Particular species of fish frequent certain spots. For instance, Tautog (*Tautoga onitis*) like to hover behind rocks where there are slight whirlpools caused by the currents and dart after their food as it comes by. Also, I believe that some of these fish hover in any given area because there also might be more oxygen where there is turbulence."

8. Kottak (1966:217) suggests that loss of this acute vision is an ideological rationale which justifies retirement owing to old age and still allows old sea captains to command the respect of younger fishermen. However, such justification is not necessary in Coqueiral, where old men are rewarded with sizable pensions for retiring.

9. E. Lowe Pierce, in a personal communication, states: ". . . you have to align your points quite precisely and remember just how they are aligned. It takes practice to become expert at this—but with practice you can mark a spot well."

10. The minimum importance that Kottak (1966) attributes to distinct fishing spots in Arembepe may well be due to the relatively few vessels (about 35) which fish from that port in an expanse of ocean equal to that utilized by more than one hundred vessels in Coqueiral.

11. Unfortunately, no studies of marine ecology have been carried out along this stretch of coastline, and fish populations are unknown.

12. "Many coastal fisheries afford relatively few good fishing spots, depending as they do upon advantageous reefs or banks . . . since such natural advantages for fishing are often scarce, the more vessels there are fishing, the less the efficiency of each vessel" (H. Gordon Scott, quoted in Bottomanne 1959:127).

13. Bottomanne (1959:12) writes: "Development of the fishing industry is largely a race with the decrease in productivity per unit, which prevents them from accumulating much wealth." Any general increase in fishing causes a decrease in catches per fishing unit.

VI. DISTRIBUTION AND REDISTRIBUTION

1. A detailed description of the regional marketing system in Northeast Brazil and a typology of Market Places can be found in Forman and Riegelhaupt (1970).

2. Informants' accounts credit the women of Coqueiral with having killed some eight soldiers from Guaiamu who attacked the village while the fishermen were at sea.

3. Salt produced in Coqueiral is not processed. Fishermen prefer to buy processed salt outside rather than to invest their labor in crushing it.

4. The loss of weight on eviscerated fish is estimated at one kilo in ten on very large fish and 200 grams apiece on small fish. Fresh fish are weighed whole unless they are very large, in which case they are first eviscerated.

VII. PATTERNS OF OWNERSHIP

1. The only holidays observed by all fishermen in the village were Good Friday, St. Peter's Day (June 29), and Brazilian Independence Day (September 7).

2. This statement, from a personal communication of Neil Boyle, RITA, state of Alagoas, was reported in an unpublished study by Dean Claxton, Department of Agricultural Economics at Berkeley (c. 1964). The project was part of a feasibility study for the establishment of a saw mill in the county of São Miguel dos Campos, Alagoas.

VIII. CREDIT, CAPITAL, AND SAVINGS

1. There are four syndromes typically related to protein deficiency.

Kwashiorkor, which has been well documented among children in tropical regions including Brazil (Waterlow and Vergara 1956), manifests the following general symptoms: edema (distended stomach), stunted growth, alterations in hair and skin color, and also ulcerations, diarrhea, anemia, dental caries, wasted muscles, apathy, and irritability (Wilson, Fisher, and Fuqua 1959:70; Davidson, Meikeljohn, and Passmore 1959:400–401).

2. Beans afford approximately 22 grams of protein per 100 grams of edible portion, as opposed to approximately 19 grams of protein per 100 grams of edible portion of second-class species of fish (INCAP-INCNND 1961).

X. CONCLUSION

1. For further discussion of Foster's position see Bennett (1966), Foster (1966), Kaplan and Saler (1966), Kennedy (1966), and Piker (1966).

2. Foster offers no explanation for the existence of peasant communities and seems to say that they exist by very virtue of their being. "Only by being conservative can peasant societies continue to exist as peasant societies" (1965:310). Yet, when seen historically and in terms of the larger universe, their genesis and their reason for continuing into the twentieth century are apparent.

3. This contradicts Foster's assertion that ". . . the average peasant sees little or no relationship between work and production techniques, on the one hand, and the acquisition of wealth, on the other. Rather, wealth is seen by villagers in the same light as land: present, circumscribed by absolute limits, and having no relationship to work" (1965:298).

4. Nevertheless, successful mobility requires at least some degree of aloofness from the problems of one's kinsmen. In one instance a local bigwig went so far as to change his name in order to avoid obligations to kinsmen with whom he temporarily severed ties. It is interesting to note that once he was firmly established he began again to involve himself with his kinsmen, who adopted his new name as their own.

5. Foster writes ". . . it logically follows from the Image of Limited Good that each minimal social unit (often the nuclear family and, in many situations, a single individual) sees itself in perpetual, unrelenting struggle with its fellows for possession of or control over what it considers to be its share of scarce values" (1965:302). The notion of an "unrelenting struggle" between minimal units fails to account for the overwhelming body of evidence in the anthropological literature that reports a tremendous amount of cooperation in peasant societies.

6. The specifics of McClelland's complex psychological construct need not occupy us here, nor should the many questions concerning methodology and interpretation that his lengthy proposition entails. In essence, the need for Achievement refers to an individual's evaluation of his per-

formance according to some standard of excellence. In this regard, there can be no doubt that *n* Achievement should be measured within a particular sociocultural frame of reference.

7. Firth (1961:109) notes that "when a new economic possibility does arrive, such as the advent of a new market for agricultural producers or for the services of middlemen, some individuals show more initiative, energy, and skill than others in taking advantage of it." We have seen that experimentation with new techniques begins first with urban elites and then spreads downward and outward toward the villages (Foster 1962:29). It would be a serious mistake, however, to consider culture change as a simple acculturative process (Murphy 1964). Urban areas offer more economic stimulus to change, and elites—first in urban areas and then along the lines of communication in rural areas—are in the most favorable position to take advantage of it.

8. Not only will values about drive and initiative and the directions these should take vary within the context of different sociocultural systems, they are also likely to vary in relation to class standing. Thus, Rosen tells us that there is a direct relationship between achievement motivation and social class in Brazil and that the higher the class position, the higher the motivation (1962:345). It is interesting to mention that in a footnote to a later paper Rosen writes, "Whatever the causes, São Paulo's growth indicates that economic growth can take place even when achievement motivation and achievement values are not pronounced among the general population . . ." (1964:344). In my view, a close examination of the historical and sociological accounts of the growth of the city of São Paulo will surely provide the variables necessary to a proper discussion of the causes of that metropolis' development.

Index

Achievement motivation, in Brazil, 137. *See also* "Need for Achievement"

Adoption, 108

Agency for the Development of the Northeast. *See* SUDENE

Agricultural colony (Palmeira): produces fruit juice and jelly, 26; weekly market at, 32, 88

Agriculture: accumulation of wealth from, 24, 26, 34; adequate land area for, 22–23, 73; difficulties in, 22–23; historical importance of, 19; as primary occupation, 112–13; soil for, 22; topography and land use, 21–26; subsistence and, 101, 146n8. *See also* Agricultural colony; Coconuts; Land tenure and land use; Markets; Sugar cane production; Wage labor

Alcohol. *See* Sugar cane production, rum

Amazon region, 9, 15; and supply of logs, 10

Animal husbandry: and agriculture, 24; cattle, 19, 21; economic importance of, 24, 116–17, 126, 135; raising of livestock, 21

Apprenticeship, 71, 94

Associação Beneficente de Coqueiral (Benevolent Society of Coqueiral). *See* Credit and Loan Association; Cooperatives

Authority within kin group, 108. *See also* Politics

Bait: breeding tank for, 124, 127–30; catching of, 53, 56, 58, 82; cost of, 58, 60, 97; importance of, 22, 58; suppliers, 60

Balsa. *See* Jangada wood

Basketry. *See* Straw industry; Women

Beach seines: economics of, 47–48; owners of, 48; repair of, 48; shore crew needed for, 50–51; size and structure of, 47–48; use of, 7, 50–51, 52, 64

Benevolent Society of Coqueiral. *See* Credit and Loan Association. *See also* Cooperatives; SUDENE

Bigwigs: capital controlled by, 36; description of 34–35, 118; example of, 37–38, 44; exploitation of fishermen by, 33, 39, 84–85, 87, 122, 133, 136; and investment, 45; oppose innovation by fishermen, 127, 136; and politics, 36, 39, 43, 44, 136

—attitudes of: toward fishermen, 84, 101, 119, 123, 126–27, 130, 132, 136, 150n2; toward planters, 119, 123. *See also* Consumption; Debts; Entrepreneurs; Politics; Wage labor

Botes, 61–64, 93–99 *passim*; life expectancy of, 94; production records for, 75, 78–80; size and construction of, 62

Brazilian currency, value of, 145n1. *See also* Cost of living

Breeding tank. *See* Bait; SUDENE

Canoes: plank, 7; difficulties in use of, 53–54; used for fishing, 9, 15

Capital: accumulation of, 12, 33, 47, 104, 111, 114, 115, 123, 125, 126,

Capital—*Continued*
135; drawn off from local community, 33; drawn from fishermen, 45,
109, 110, 122; and investment, 45,
46, 53, 104, 125. *See also* Entrepreneurs; Investment

Captains: role of, 70; in seine fishing,
51; and share of catch, 82, 123–24.
See also Fishing spots; Pensions

Cast nets, 6; description of, 58; use in
onshore fishing, 7

Catch: division of, 51, 52, 81, 82, 83,
91; importance of, in choice of fishing strategies, 15

Catholic Church, 32; custom of donat-
ing fish to, 43; as landowner, 22, 24,
44

Change, resistance to: and incentive, 34;
and opposition of bigwigs, 55; and social stratification, 118–19; theoretical
basis for, 13, 16. *See also* "Image of
Limited Good;" Price controls

Children: as economic boon, 108; foster
care of, 108–109. *See also* Adoption;
Apprentices; Straw industry

Class consciousness, 137–38

Coastal survey, 9

Coconuts: commercial value of, 24–25;
and land use, 23; and social stratification, 34. *See also* Agriculture; Inheritance; Investment

Colônia de Pescadores. See Fishermen's
guild

Colonization: and fishing, 10; and social
structure, 11. *See also* Portuguese

Commerce. *See* Stores; Markets

Communication: contact by sea, history of, 17, 19; lines of, 31–33

Competition, 73, 136; for limited market, 90; minimized, 74

Conservation: as rational response, 16,
119, 137; cognitive exploration of
132; economic and sociological factors in, 137; and problem of limited
means, 135, 138; psychological explanation of, 136. *See also* Achievement; Cooperation; "Image of Limited Good"

Consumption, 32, 84, 108–109, 110,
114–15, 116; of fishermen, 110; of
local bigwigs, 36, 110–11. *See also*
Fuel; Stores

Continental shelf, 7–8, 61. *See also*
Fishing grounds

Cooperation: alleged lack of, 37, 42,
119; of fishermen, 101, 106, 108, 110,
122, 129, 135, 136; indispensable in
peasant economy, 39, 105, 135, 136;
in net fishing, 50. *See also* Crews;
Idleness

Cooperative selling, failure of, 92

Cost of living, 4. *See also* Consumption; Inflation

Craft: changes in type of, 12, 14, 15–
16; ecological factors in choice of, 7,
9. See also *Botes*; Fishing; Hull sailboats; Jangadas; *Paquetes*

Credit, 111, 114, 135; for consumption
goods, 110, 111; control over sources
of, 34; difficult to obtain, 40, 45, 55,
111, 118, 119, 126, 127

Credit and Loan Association (Associação Beneficente do P. de C.): administration of, 43–44; corruption in,
44, 128, 129; formation of, 43; and
politics, 129, 130

Crews: as occupational category, 102;
and income, 13, 97, 100; maintenance of, 71, 101, 103, 123; membership in, 13, 50–51, 55, 102, 122;
shore (*see* Beach seines)

Debts, 108; of bigwigs, 36; of peasants,
36, 109, 111; of middlemen, 91; payment of, 111, 126

Diet: quality of, 98, 108–109, 110,
148n2, 150n1, 151n2; subsistence,
21–22, 28, 57. *See also* Malnutrition

Diffusion, of fishing techniques: explanations of, lacking in depth, 8–9. *See
also* Foster, George

Diminishing returns: law of, applied to
fishing, 72, 73, 150n13; in lobster
fishing, 14

Distribution. *See* Markets

Division of catch. *See* Catch, division of

Drunkenness, 106. *See also* Sugar cane production, rum

Earnings: drained off through taxes, 40, 45, 109; of fishermen, 4, 24, 47, 51, 55, 73, 75–80, 99–100, 104, 105, 107, 109, 119–20, 124–25; of fish hawkers, 88–89, 105; and incentives of share system, 83, 124; limited by price controls, 39; and occupational distribution, 27–28; of women, 27–28, 106, 111, 114. *See also* Wage labor

Ecological factors: in choice of craft, 7, 9; and fishing strategies, 9, 46, 61; in location of fishing spots, 72, 150n10; in price of logs, 10; and social change, 12, 131, 136–37

Economic controls, 33, 39, 84–85, 87. *See also* Bigwigs; Capital; Credit; Social control

Economic organization: changes in, 11, 13; in the county, 26–31

Education, 32, 36, 38, 110

Employment. *See* Idleness; Migration; Occupational distribution; Wage labor

Entrepreneurs, 57–58, 60, 92, 99, 103, 122, 123–24, 125, 134, 137; control labor, 14, 122; control production, 12, 47; historical limits of, 11; and innovation, 6, 12, 13, 15–16; women as, 114. *See also* Middlemen; Risk

Family: constitution of, 105, 107–108; as economic unit, 47, 83, 86, 102–103, 104, 105–107, 108, 114–15, 131, 135. *See also* Kinship; Women

Fishermen's guild, 37, 40; administration of, 40–41; failings of, 40, 42; fishermen's resentment of, 41, 43; income and expenditures of, 41, 43; and loans, 109; membership in, 39, 41–42. *See also* Nepotism

Fish hawkers, 84, 85, 123; earnings of, 88–89; expenditures of, 90; and family obligations, 13, 85–86, 87; licenses and fees required of, 39, 42;

preference for male hawkers, 86; relationship with fishermen, 85, 124. *See also* Risk

Fishing: and agriculture, 23; for albacore, 14; basic patterns of, 61, 68; Japanese, and tuna fishing, 7; Peruvian fishing industry and modernization, 8; as predominant economic activity, 26–27; primitive methods of, 47, 74; productivity, 13, 75–80, 115–16; seasonal patterns of, 62–65; types of, 7, 17, 46. *See also* Craft; Portuguese; Seasons

Fishing economy: changes in, 7–8, 12, 146n7; government legislation concerning, 10; importance of, in community, 26–27; part economy, 10; traditional aspects of, 12

Fishing grounds: boundaries of, 65, 73; distribution of fish within, 68, 149n6; extent of, 73; generalized knowledge about, 65–66, 68, 71, 149n4; location of, 66–68, 70–71, 72; mapping of, 66; opening up of new, 15

Fishing seasons, 62–65, 115–16

Fishing spots: importance of, 70; location of, by landmarks, 65–66, 67, 68, 148n3; secrecy of, 71, 72, 136; specialized knowledge of captains of, 70, 71, 124, 149n9. *See also* Ecological factors

Fishing strategies: customary alternation of, 61, 80, 85, 102, 123; differential access to, 47; factors affecting, 62, 81, 103–104, 134; preference for rafts, 83, 93, 101, 133. *See also* Independent production

Fishing zones, 6, 66; Northeast Fishing Zone, 7

Food supply, 10, 12, 118, 119; importance of region as source of, 19, 22; from mangrove swamp, 21. *See also* Diet; Subsistence; Stores

Foster, George: *Culture and Conquest: America's Spanish Heritage*, cited, 8. *See also* Conservatism; "Image of Limited Good"

Fuel, 4; from mangrove swamp, 21; type used, as indicator of rank, 110
Fund of rent, 145n3

Gill nets, 53–55, 119, 122; acceptance of, 119–20; division of catch of, 55; economics of, 54–55; use of, opposed by bigwigs, 55, 119

Handicrafts. *See* Straw industry
Hull sailboats: introduction of, to Coqueiral, 122, 123–27; replace indigenous rafts, 9, 14; resistance to, 12–13, 16; use along northeast coast, 7, 104. *See also* Change; Portuguese

Idleness: causes family squabbles, 106; example of, 38; of fishermen, 15, 105; myth of, perpetuated by bigwigs, 36, 119
"Image of Limited Good," 131–32, 136, 151n1-4
Independent production: preference for, 13, 15, 93, 99, 100, 103, 104, 119, 122–23, 124, 133; and resistance to change, 14, 15, 119. *See also* Change; Fishing strategies
Indians: Caeté, 17, 19; pre-Columbian economy, 10; Potiguars, 17; role of, in fishing economy, 11; Tupinambá, 7, 19
Inflation, 33, 110
Inheritance, 23; of coconut groves, 24; of fishing equipment, 31
Innovation, 6; and capital formation, 33, 116–17, 125, 135; of gill nets, 53, 119; and individual motivations, 16, 36, 100, 119, 122, 125, 133, 134, 137, 152n7; rejection of, 118, 131, 134; and social status, 36, 118, 119, 123, 124, 133, 136
Interest rates, 44, 114, 122
Investment, 6, 118, 125; decisions concerning, 108, 114, 131, 134; lack of, in fishing economy, 33, 45, 102, 135; in livestock, 116, 126. *See also* Capital

Jangadas, 5–6, 12, 61–64, 93–105 *passim*; advantages of, 5–6; construction of, 5, 62; counted, 94; origin of name, 3; types of, 61–64, 93–105 *passim*. *See also* Botes; *Jangadas de alto; Paquetes*
Jangadas de alto, 12, 61–64, 93–105 *passim*; construction and size of, 5, 12, 62; life expectancy of, 76, 79; preferred by bigwigs, 97, 99; productivity of, 74–77
Jangada wood (*pau de jangada; piuba*): availability of, 5, 9–10, 103; and middlemen, 115, 118; properties of, 5, 6, 94. *See also* Logs; Legislation

Kinship obligations, 86, 91, 97, 100, 102, 103, 106, 107, 109, 110, 119. *See also* Family; Fish hawkers

Lambuda. See Pocket seine
Land tenure and land use, 22–23, 24; property rights, 24; on sugar plantations, 26
Legislation: hardwoods reserved for naval use, 10, 19, 146n6; in fishing economy, 10, 39, 40, 133, 145n4. *See also* Price controls; Taxation
Licenses: to fish, 39; to sell fish, 39. *See also* Legislation
Livestock. *See* Animal husbandry
Lobster fishing, 14, 57
Logs: obtained from plantations, 12; prices of, 13. *See also* Amazon region; Jangada wood

McClelland, David. *See* "Need for Achievement"
Malnutrition (protein), 108, 150n1. *See also* Diet
Mangrove swamp, 21; importance of, 22, 57. *See also* Subsistence
Marijuana, 4, 102
Marine ecology, folk conception of, 74
Maritime Institute, 27. *See also* Pensions; Legislation
Market economy, growth of, 11
Markets, 46, 88, 110, 111, 112, 150n1;

Markets—*Continued*
and fishing strategy, 61, 134; glutting of, 29, 50, 58, 90, 91–92, 135; and innovation, 6, 9, 13, 134; link to local economy, 32; supply of fish guaranteed to Guaiamu, 39, 85, 88, 119; weekly, 32, 87
Middlemen: and baiting activities, 58; in coconut economy, 24; itinerant, 89; and kin ties, 14; numbers of, 14, 85, 91, 115, 135; in straw industry, 111–12, 115. *See also* Entrepreneurs; Fish hawkers; Straw industry; Women
Migrant labor, 31, 104
Migration, 28–31, 109–10; to Coqueiral 22
Município, meaning of, 147n10. *See also* Economic organization
Mutirão, 110. *See also* Cooperation

"Need for Achievement," 136–37, 151n6, 152n8
Nepotism, 38–39, 40–41, 44
Nets. *See* Beach seines; Gill nets; Pocket seines; Subsistence

Occupational distribution, 27–28, 91, 112
Ownership, of rafts and equipment: dependent on agricultural earnings, 47; expenses involved in, 55, 83, 97, 98, 123; patterns of, 14, 97–101, 104; and share of catch, 82, 83, 134. *See also* Capital; Investment
Overfishing, 29, 73; in lobster industry, 14; prevented, 65. *See also* Fishing spots, secrecy of

Paquets, 61–64, 93–99 *passim*; advantages of, 64; life expentancy of, 94; productivity of, 75–78; size and construction of, 61–62
Patrão: paternalism of, toward peasants, 36; and social mobility, 37, 55, 119; vacuum left by, 34, 115, 118, 147n3
Peasant: definition of 143n3; economy, 11, 34–35 *passim*, 131, 132; relation-ship with bigwigs, 36, 44–45, 126–27, 132; role in market economy, 11, 134, 135
Peasant behavior. *See* Conservatism
Pensions, for retired fishermen, 27, 40, 103, 106, 129
Plantation economy, 26
Plumbing. *See* Fishing grounds, location of
Pocket seines, 52–53
Politics, local: in county seat, 32; party, 36, 37, 38, 43–44, 148n7; power of bigwigs in, 34, 43, 132–33; spoils of, 42, 44
Portuguese: fishing industry, 8; influence in Brazil, 9. *See also* Hull sailboats; Indians; Legislation
Preservation of catch, difficulties of, 58, 92. *See also* Salting process
Price controls, 104; curb incentive, 100, 123, 124; imposed on fishermen and hawkers, 39; and inflation, 33; limit profits, 87, 90, 124; resentment of, 41; setting of, 87. *See also* Legislation; Taxation
Prices: of fish, 39, 87–89, 91, 110; and innovation, 6, 13, 14; of logs, 6, 10, 14, 96, 103–104. *See also* Inflation

Rafts. *See* Botes; Jangadas; *Jangadas de alto*; *Paquetes*
Redistribution. *See* Share system
Replacement of rafts and equipment, 6, 13, 14, 45, 47, 61, 115, 117, 135
Risk, monetary, 135; in animal husbandry, 116; and bait sellers, 112; failure to assume, by outside agencies, 45; and fish hawkers, 88–90, 91, 92, 112. *See also* Earnings; Entrepreneurs; Investment; Middlemen
Rum. *See* Sugar cane production

Sails, lateen, 5, 12, 62, 145n2
Salt flats, abandoned, 21
Salting process, 62, 74; cost of, 89; effectiveness of, 90; and price of fish, 88; rafts equipped for, 5
Savings, 111, 115, 116, 135. *See also*

Savings—*Continued*
Animal husbandry; Family; Straw industry

Scarcity of fish, 90

Schools. *See* Education

Seasons, 62–65, 75–79, 90; Lenten, 63, 65, 90; summer, 63–65, 115–16; winter, 63–64

Secrecy, 65, 71, 72, 74, 136. *See also* Fishing spots

Share system, 14, 51, 55, 56, 82–84, 91, 97, 100, 102–103, 122, 123, 133, 146n7; as alternative to wage labor, 83; captain's share in, 51; in gill net fishing, 55; in lobster fishing, 14; in seine fishing, 51, 52; in shark fishing, 56; in turtle fishing, 56

Shark fishing, 56. *See also* Bait

Social mobility, 55, 112–13, 136, 137, 151n4; of bigwigs, limited, 36, 37

Social status: symbols of, 36, 136; limits of, 37–38

Social stratification, 13, 34, 118, 132. *See also* Bigwigs; *Patrão*; Peasant

Spacing mechanism. *See* Secrecy

Stores, 110, 114; inventory bought at Guaiamu market, 32; local stock of, limited, 32, 111; supplemented by traders, 32. *See also* Credit; Markets

Straw industry: children help in, 27, 115; design of baskets, 111–12; earnings from, 106–107, 114; elasticity of employment in, 27–28, 115; productivity, 112; as source of liquid capital, 111, 112, 135. *See also* Credit; Women

Subsistence, 21, 22, 28; and agriculture, 22–23, 146n8; and animal husbandry, 24; economy, 10, 19; and entrepreneurship, 57–60; and fishing, 51, 108; transformation from, to money economy, 11

SUDENE: funds for breeding tank from, 128–130; supervision of construction, 130

Sugar cane production, 19, 21, 26; mill built, 21; and planters, 147n1; records of, 26; rum from, 26, 32, 102, 111, 115. *See also* Agriculture; Land tenure and land use; Wage labor

Taxation: bigwigs benefit by, 38; on fish, 39, 84, 109; by fishermen's guild, 40–41, 42; on land, 38

Traditionalism. *See* Conservatism. *See also* Change

Transportation, 31–32

Triangulation, visual. *See* Fishing grounds; Fishing spots

Turtle fishing, 56

Upper class. See *Patrão*

Wage labor: in agriculture, 26–27; availability of, 29, 105–106, 128; exploitation of, by local bigwigs, 38, 44; in lobster fishing, 14; minimum salary for, in Alagoas, 40. *See also* Migrant labor

Women, 22, 91, 114, 115; in decision-making, 114; occupations of, 27–28, 52, 86, 87, 106, 111–12; role of, in capital accumulation, 114